The
HONEY
BEE

A BUSINESS PARABLE ABOUT GETTING UN-STUCK AND
TAKING CONTROL OF YOUR FINANCIAL FUTURE

JAKE STENZIANO & GINO BARBARO

RIVER GROVE
BOOKS

Published by River Grove Books
Austin, TX
www.rivergrovebooks.com

Distributed by River Grove Books

Design and composition by Greenleaf Book Group
Cover design by Greenleaf Book Group

Publisher's Cataloging-in-Publication data is available.

Print ISBN: 978-1-63299-242-0

eBook ISBN: 978-1-63299-243-7

Audiobook: 978-1-63299-244-4

First Edition

CONTENTS

TWO DISGRUNTLED GUYS

In 2010, life for us sucked.

Make no mistake: By some measures, things were great. We had our health and our families, and we both had jobs. Not everyone could say that.

Sometimes, however, those things just aren't enough to keep you from feeling stuck.

Stuck is exactly what we were. We both felt trapped and powerless. As the effects of the recession trickled down, Jake was stuck in a dead-end sales job where layoffs always seemed to be around the corner, and the ceiling above him felt more like a coffin lid. For Gino, *stuck* meant washing dishes in his family's restaurant, fighting a sense of being trapped forever.

Just a few short years ago that was us: the frustrated drug rep and the dissatisfied pizza guy.

We didn't know each other, but we had a lot in common. We felt powerless to control the direction of our lives. Every day meant waking up and doing work we didn't want to, then going home and hoping there'd be enough money at the end of the month. It was an endless cycle we didn't know how to change.

At the same time, we both still hoped for something better. We dreamed of a time when we wouldn't have to worry about money, wouldn't dread going to work in the morning, a time when *we* were leading our lives, instead of our lives leading *us*.

The problem was that we weren't sure how to make any of that happen.

Things finally reached a turning point when, in desperation, Jake decided to leave New York for Tennessee. At least there he figured life would be more affordable.

As always, luck seems to follow action, and it was then that Jake met Gino, who was still washing dishes and trying to save his family business from the grip of the recession.

Gino told Jake about his dream of investing in multifamily real estate properties. Jake shared his plans of moving somewhere more affordable, where he could try to invest in something that would help him escape his sales job.

That was when the light bulb lit up.

There we were, two disgruntled guys, both wanting to

create passive income, both wanting to take control of our lives—both unsure how to do it alone.

That was when our partnership was born. Not long after, we bought our first investment property—a mom-and-pop—owned apartment building with a few units. The drug rep and the pizza guy were now in business!

Fast-forward to today, and "stuck" is the last word that comes to mind. Our humble beginnings have spawned thousands of real estate units, worth tens of millions of dollars. Our initial apartments have spun off businesses in property management, construction, education, and more.

Best of all, we're in control of our lives. Our approach to multiple streams of income has allowed us to secure our financial future, and create something that still gets us out of bed in the morning feeling excited. No more dreading the day ahead, no more feeling powerless. It's difficult to imagine going back to relying on just one source of income, feeling powerless, being *afraid*.

The Multiple Streams of Income (MSI) approach has given us security that would be difficult to find any other way, and it's perfectly aligned with our vision of creating generational wealth for our families. It's no exaggeration to say that having multiple streams of income has completely transformed our lives, the lives of those around us.

When we started, we had no idea what we were embarking upon. That's really the problem, isn't it? Not knowing is *scary*. And that keeps you stuck, afraid to take action because you don't know what to do.

We wrote this book to change that.

The story that follows is our way of passing on what we wish we had known when we started. It's a way to share the shortcuts, secrets, and principles you need to take the first step toward building multiple streams of income, and creating a life where you feel in charge.

No matter what your job is, or what your dreams are, we think having multiple streams of income is the best possible way to escape the rat race and take control of your life. It's a path forward that anyone can follow, and it's our hope that this book lights the way.

After all, if a drug rep and a pizza guy can do it, why can't you?

To the first stream,

Jake Stenziano & Gino Barbaro

But First . . .

Dear Reader,

This is a work of fiction. The characters in this book aren't real. But the lessons the book teaches? They're very real—we've seen them work time and time again.

So, yes: This may be only a story, but if there were ever a tale that could come true, this is it.

—Jake & Gino

1

THE BEEKEEPER

When the tire blows, I'm composing my resignation letter in my head.

It's become my favorite way to pass the time on long drives, and this stretch is a particularly painful one. I don't know if it's the potholes or the lack of anything to look at but trees, but the further I drive, the less happy I am.

No doubt that's why I'm in a darker mood than usual, and debating whether to open the letter with *Dear Asshat*, or *To the Douchebags Whom It May Concern*. Both have their appeal, and both are, as far as I'm concerned, true.

I've found that the take-this-job-and-shove-it fantasy is particularly helpful on bad days. And this is definitely one of those. Not only am I going home empty-handed, but it's also bucketing rain, which is going to make a terrible drive just that much longer. It just gives me more time to dwell on a job I can barely tolerate, but from which I can never seem to escape.

When the tire goes, I'm so deep in the daydream of quitting that it takes me a moment to realize what's happened. Before my brain connects the dots between the loud noise and the sudden sideways lurch of the car, the back end is already breaking loose on the wet pavement.

I fight the skid, pulling the wheel first one way, then the other as the car fishtails wildly. Through the blur of the wet windshield, the pickets of a guardrail sweep through my vision.

In a heart-pounding few seconds, it's over. I limp the car to the shoulder. There's a wobbling, scraping noise from the back that doesn't sound good. I squint through the rain, over the guardrail: It looks like a drop.

I loosen my fingers from their death grip on the wheel and take a deep breath. *That was close.* Just a few extra feet and I might have been upside down at the bottom of a ravine. For the first time today, I feel lucky.

It makes me realize how stupid the job-quitting daydream is. I'm never going to do it, so why do I bother? It's like one of those dreams where you win the lottery. When you wake up broke, you just feel even worse than usual. I should just feel grateful to be right-side up on the highway, my heart still beating.

My heart slows and I slump back in the seat. The rain splatters the windshield in between the thumping sweeps of the wipers. My feeling of gratitude fades as quickly as it came. *Not a good day*, I think.

—

I pull my roadside assistance card from my wallet. There's no point in changing my own tire in this weather. I check my phone. No service. *Great.*

Outside, the rain is still coming down. I don't have a raincoat or an umbrella, just my suit jacket. It's better than nothing, so I throw it on, pop the trunk, and step out of the car into the rain.

The trunk, of course, is a jumbled mess of sample cases and crap, and by the time I get things shoved around enough to get at the spare tire, I know that the suit jacket actually *isn't* better than nothing. It's the same as nothing. I'm soaked right through.

When I finally discover that the spare is flat, I'm beyond frustrated. I scream into the gray, rainy sky, and slam the trunk lid. I climb back into the driver's seat, sit in a puddle of water, and wonder, *Why me?*

—

Things didn't start out this way. In the beginning, my job selling medical supplies was great. The pay was high. Training was a priority. There were lots of perks and elaborate company events. I felt this sense of upward mobility—of *possibility*.

For a while, the job was every salesperson's dream: high margin, steady demand, and a product that helps people. What more could you want?

I found out pretty quickly when the company abruptly changed hands. It turns out there's a lot to want. You can want a job where they don't change your territory just when you've finally built some decent relationships. Where they don't change the commission structure every time you feel like you're starting to make a buck. Where your best customers don't get clawed back and become corporate accounts as soon as your hard work starts to pay off.

Now, the whole thing feels like one big bait and switch. And yet I keep showing up every day. On the worst days, like today, I write my resignation letter in my head. But then I show up the next day like some sucker in a rigged carnival game.

Part of it is the carrot: They keep dangling an account executive title just out of my reach. That would mean more money and less time on the road, which would be great news for both me and my wife, Emma.

The other reason I keep showing up—the thing opposite the carrot—is the stick. I *can't* leave. I need the money. I don't have a fancy degree or fancy connections. I don't have a fancy trust fund. What I do have is a fancy mortgage that we can barely afford. Leaving feels like financial suicide.

I can't stay. I can't leave. I chase the carrots, but they're always dangled just out of reach. I fear the stick, which makes me feel trapped. I feel like I'm getting nowhere.

There's a loud *crack* of thunder, and lightning brightens the gray afternoon. Despite it all, I laugh. Right now, I literally *am* getting nowhere. I check my phone again. No signal.

I'm about to get out and start walking when a car pulls up behind me, its headlights washing over me in the rain-darkened afternoon. I squint in the rearview mirror, but I can't see anything in the glare.

The headlights turn off, and I realize it's not a car, but a pickup truck. One that's seen better days, from what I can tell. I'm about to hop out and save whoever it is the trouble of getting out into the rain, but they beat me to it.

I say *they*, because there's no way to tell whether the person climbing out of the pickup truck is a man or a woman. They're shrouded from the neck down in a bulky white suit, topped with a sort of floppy white helmet. For the briefest moment, I wonder if I'm about to be abducted by aliens. *Sure, Noah. An alien in a beat-up old Ford.*

Okay. So it's not aliens. But what's with the spacesuit? A darker thought strikes me: *What if it's a serial killer?* The spacesuit looks like one of those white forensic outfits psychopaths use to keep from leaving evidence.

Suddenly, my crappy sales job doesn't seem so crappy. Suddenly, I'd give anything to be back on the road and feeling grateful for my ever-shrinking commission check.

A white-gloved hand knocks on my window.

I push the button, lowering it a crack too small to let in rain or aliens or serial killers.

"Well hello," says the warm, slightly raspy voice of an older man. "You look like a fella in need of a better day."

—

A few moments later, I'm tucked into the warm cab of the old pickup truck, with most of my thoughts of aliens and serial killers left behind. The truck is at least three decades old, but it's clean and seems to be idling smoothly.

"Thanks so much," I say. "There's no cell service here. My spare is flat. I guess I need a tow."

The man pulls the strange white helmet off his head, and I see that it isn't a helmet at all, but more of a floppy hat with mesh over the front. Underneath the getup is a man who looks to be in his late 60s. Fit, with a healthy but lined face. One that shows its years but carries them well.

"I had a spare like that once," he says, setting down the hat. I think he's joking, but I can't really tell. Then he looks directly at me and I see the twinkle in his eyes.

"Tom Barnham," he says, pulling off a white glove and extending a hand.

"Noah Mason," I reply. "Thank you again. Is there a phone near here I could use?"

Tom shifts the truck into gear, and we pull away. "Yessir," he says. "We'll have to go to my place, though. Nearest cell tower is a ways off."

I watch out the passenger window as we drive past my car, and I feel another pang of uncertainty.

"Don't worry," Tom says. "Your car will be fine here." He tugs at the zipper that extends down the front of his white jumpsuit.

"What's with the outfit?" I ask.

"It's for the bees," he says.

"The bees?"

"Was just on my way to pick up a hive when the storm came in," he explains. "Otherwise you might be sharing this ride with a few thousand other hitchhikers."

"You're a beekeeper?"

Tom seems to ponder this. "After a fashion," he says. "Although you might better say *they* keep *me*."

I don't quite get this, but before I can ask what he means, the old truck's engine sputters and then backfires. I wonder if I'm about to be stranded for a second time at the side of the road.

"Don't worry," Tom says. "She's never let me down."

—

As promised, the old truck runs smoothly. I feel strangely relaxed, despite the day, and find myself happily chatting with Tom. After a few minutes, I realize I've been rambling on.

The truck backfires again. *I guess there's not much money in bees, I think. It would take a lot of honey to buy a new car.*

Then the truck slows, we turn into an opening in the trees, and I abruptly change my mind.

2

THE HONEY TRAP

The transition is so fast it's almost disorienting. One moment we're driving a washboard country road, staring at a tangle of forest, the next I'm on an immaculately maintained laneway, curving through what must be 20 acres or more of perfect green lawn. The crushed limestone laneway rises in a series of small hills across the estate. Perfectly manicured trees spaced in even intervals run along each side of the lane.

To either side, wide expanses of lawn stretch away to a distant tree line. To the left, a wide river winds its way along the edge of the clearing before tumbling into a small lake. A group of deer feeds in the trees along the water's edge.

On the right, a carved wooden sign reads: TRIBUTARY ACRES.

As we crest the slight rise of the driveway, I immediately see the source of the name: A half-dozen or more small streams emerge from the trees to carve a winding path downhill, then merge to form the river that flows down to where the deer stand, grazing.

Ahead, the road curves and then rises again. There, at the top of the estate grounds, a sprawling modern building perches at the edge of the hill, its front face almost entirely glass.

The house itself is huge, but it's been carefully designed to nestle into the hill, fitting into the contours of the land, rising in some areas, falling in others. At one point, the grounds flow over an entire level, creating a living roof under which nestles an enormous glass-fronted atrium. Long strands of flowered vines and greenery sway over the edges, and I can see the quick movements of birds darting from one bloom to the next.

As if to emphasize the contrast, the old Ford backfires loudly before continuing to chug up the hill.

The laneway curves beneath the glass walls of the home, and climbs again to emerge behind the house, where a bay of garage doors stand open to the sun, which has just begun to break free from the clouds.

Each bay contains a car, and I recognize many—ranging from the exotic to the practical. A classic 1950s convertible sparkles next to a new SUV. A sleek, futuristic roadster lurks beside a pair of motorcycles. One bay stands empty. Tom pulls the old pickup inside and shuts off the engine.

"Home sweet home," he says.

My mouth simply hangs open. *Sweet indeed. Maybe there's money in bees after all.*

—

Tom steps out of his white bee suit, hangs it on a hook, and then leads me through a door, where we emerge on a high walkway overlooking the enormous glass-fronted atrium I saw from the drive. It's a huge, open space—kitchen, living room, dining room and more, all in one cavernous room.

It's beautifully decorated, but my eyes are drawn to the glass wall that spans the entire front of the space. The view is incredible. An infinity pool sparkles in front, and beyond that, the grass rolls in waves down to the river.

In the distance, the last of the storm moves across a series of low mountain ranges. The clouds have mostly departed, and the sun's rays scatter in humid beams across the sky.

Wow.

"The rain's over," Tom says. "Let's open this place up."

He walks to a long bar at one side of the room. He picks up a tablet from the bar top and slides his finger along the screen. There's a soft *click*, then a whirring sound. I turn toward the sound and watch in awe as the entire glass wall begins to slide open. Within moments, the room is open to the outside. A warm breeze blows in, waving the greenery that hangs from the mouth of what now feels like a bright, modern cavern.

I'm so captivated by the sight that I don't even hear Tom call the tow truck on my behalf.

"Earl says he'll be a couple of hours yet," he says, coming out from behind the bar. "Apparently you're not the only one in need of a tow."

I manage to tear my eyes away from the view long enough to thank Tom again for his rescue efforts.

"Don't mention it. You're just lucky I didn't have a truck-load of bees," he jokes.

I'd almost forgotten about the bees.

"Earlier," I say, "when we were in the truck, you mentioned that you were a beekeeper, but the bees keep *you*. What did you mean?"

Tom doesn't reply, but stands with me and stares out over the green expanse of lawn.

"Starting to clear up," he says at last. "Feel like giving me a hand with something?"

——

Ten minutes later, I'm in a white bee suit of my own, and Tom and I are back in the old Ford, bumping our way down a dirt road that leads from behind the house to a stand of trees in the distance.

As we reach the tree line, I can see there's a small barn

nestled into the edge of the forest. Like the Ford, it's old but well maintained. We step out of the truck into the sun, and I stare back at the elegant home a ways behind us.

"You have a beautiful spot here," I say.

"Alice and I spent a long time planning the place," he says.

"I don't mean to pry, but . . . is all this from selling honey?"

For the first time, I think I've surprised Tom. His eyes widen, and then he throws back his head and laughs.

"Hell, no."

"Oh." I smile awkwardly. "And the name? Tributary Acres? I guess that's named after all those rivers flowing together?"

"Well, yes and no," Tom said. "As it happens, Alice and I had the name picked out before we even found the place. Finding those streams on the property did pretty much seal the deal, though."

"You already knew the name?"

"My business is called Tributary, Inc. We always figured we'd name our retirement home after it—what with the business paying for it all."

"Why tributary?" I ask.

I follow Tom to the barn, and he pulls open an old wooden door.

"I named the business after my philosophy," he says. "I was always a believer in multiple streams of income. Tributary is just a fancy name for stream."

Tom steps inside the barn, and I follow him into the gloom. As my eyes adjust, I can see the place is full of old farm implements and tools. In one corner, a towering stack of hay bales leans against the wall. Tom walks to a tool bench and begins to root around beneath it.

"Multiple streams of income," I say. "Like having more than one job?"

"Not exactly," Tom says. "Although a job is certainly one stream."

He pulls a wooden crate from beneath the bench. A number of tools protrude from it, including what looks like a tin teapot.

"Most people rely on one source of income," Tom says. "That one source is usually their job. Every week, they get a paycheck—that's money that flows into their account. As long as they keep showing up at work every day, that one stream of money will keep flowing."

Tom hands me the crate, and we walk back outside into the sunlight.

"When it comes to streams," Tom continues, "some have better jobs than others. A doctor might have a bigger stream than a mechanic. The mechanic might have a bigger stream than a barista. But they all share one thing in common: Their entire life depends on one stream. If they stop working, the stream stops flowing. They work to serve the stream. They don't have any choice. In those cases, that one stream can become a prison."

That's exactly what my job feels like, I thought.

Tom walks toward the back of the barn, and I follow behind, my bee suit flapping at my legs. Behind the barn is a small clearing. At the furthest edge lies a collection of wooden boxes with lids that I recognize from photographs. They're bee boxes. Manmade hives.

Tom stops and takes the crate of tools from me.

"In many ways," he says, "bees are like those folks with one job. They're hard workers, gathering pollen and nectar day after day. There are thousands of bees in a hive, each one working to keep the honey flowing. If they stop, the honey stops. It's like a company full of workers. The bees show up every day. They work like hell, and the honey flows."

"Sounds like an honest day's work," I say.

"Sure," Tom says, "and for the bees, I reckon it's fine. They have enough to live on. They have a predictable job to do every day."

Tom motions for me to put my bee hat on.

"But the real winner," he says, pulling on his own hat over his head, "is the guy that owns the hive."

—

Tom bends to the crate and pulls out the tin teapot. Now I see it looks more like the Tin Man's hat in *The Wizard of Oz*. Like an upside down metal funnel on top of a can.

Tom opens a hatch in the side of the can and stuffs in some dry, grass-like material from the crate. He lights it with a match. After a moment, he closes the hatch. Then, a tiny swirl of smoke seeps from the spout of the teapot.

"What's that for?" I ask.

There's a flat panel on the side of the pot, and Tom pushes it gently. A poof of smoke jets out of the teapot spout.

"It's a bee smoker," he says. "A critical piece of beekeeping equipment."

We walk to the hives, and I begin to hear a low buzzing noise. I feel a little uncertainty creep over me. Again, Tom seems to sense it.

"Don't worry," he says. "You'll be fine."

He approaches one of the boxes and uses the smoker to gently fog the beehive, spreading smoke underneath and around the box.

"Come closer," he says.

I walk up behind him, and he gently lifts the lid off the hive. The buzz grows in volume. Inside, *thousands* of bees crawl over vertical boards that stand inside the bee box. As I look closer, I realize the boards are like big honeycombs, pocked with perfectly symmetrical little octagons. Everywhere I look, there are bees crawling this way and that. The low buzz grows.

"Wow." It's all I can say. It's truly amazing.

"At least ten thousand bees in there," Tom says.

I'm mesmerized.

"Something, isn't it?" Tom says. "I've been doing this for years, and it still amazes me. The more time I spend keeping bees, the more I learn."

His voice takes on a dreamlike tone. "It might surprise you," he says quietly, "but just about everything I know about how to build streams of income, I learned from bees."

"From *bees*?" I ask.

"Bees have a lot to teach you—about what to do *and* what not to. It's all in there."

Tom reaches gently into the box and slides one of the combs up where I can see it. A few of the bees take flight, but most are busy crawling over the honeycomb.

"They've been busy," Tom says. "I'll be harvesting the honey soon."

I look at the bees, crawling across the comb, over and over. "Why don't they leave?"

Tom slides the comb back in place. "They're protecting the honey," he says. "It's what they've worked for. It keeps them alive, helps them build the hive. Without a supply of honey, the hive will die."

Tom carefully places the lid back on the bee box.

"Think of honey as *money* to bees," Tom says. "They work hard, they create things, and the honey is the reward. It's the raw material they need to survive and prosper—just like money is to us. Bees leaving honey would be like you walking away from your paycheck."

"I wish," I say. It comes out of my mouth before I even realize it.

Tom looks at me intently. "Do you?" he asks, after a moment.

I can feel my face redden under the bee hat. "I am a little frustrated," I admit. "I guess I'm like a bee. I can't walk away from the honey."

Rather than being sympathetic, Tom seems delighted by this.

"Exactly," he says. "That's what I call 'the honey trap.' As the honey comes in, you end up doing things with the honey. Like the bees, perhaps you add more mouths to feed. The mouths consume more. You need more hive space. More hive space means more mouths, more honey."

"Like my mortgage," I say. "It's like a big hive that takes a lot of honey to operate."

"Bingo," he says. "That's the honey trap."

Something occurs to me. "If the honey is so important, why didn't the bees attack us?"

"Ah," Tom says. "That's where the smoker comes in. When the smoke enters the hive, it masks the signals that bees send to each other about danger. That way they don't get riled up."

Tom walks back toward the crate.

"The smoke also triggers the bees to feed on honey—they think there might be a fire. It's sort of the bee equivalent of grabbing all your valuables when your house is burning."

Tom takes his bee hat off, and I do the same.

"There's a kind of smoke in our everyday lives that makes us behave the same," he says.

"How so?"

"We have a tendency to get fogged," Tom replies. "By our upbringing, society, our employers. The expectations of a *culture*. The lure and allure of what that next batch of honey can buy."

I think of our fancy house. About how I keep writing those resignation letters over and over.

"Are you saying I'm being fooled?" I ask.

"Maybe not intentionally," Tom says. "When you go to your job each day, you're not faced with a burning building. But there's a kind of smoke that's doing something very similar. There's a fog of sorts—it makes you complacent. It dulls your sense of danger."

I laugh. "My job's not exactly dangerous."

"Depends on how you define danger," Tom says. "Let's say I use a different word. Instead of danger, think *risk*."

"I wouldn't say my job is risky either," I say.

Tom opens the little hatch in the side of the bee smoker and dumps out the last of the burning embers onto the ground. The tiny coals begin to smoke in the dry grass at our feet.

"Let's say you were to stay the rest of your life in this job," Tom says. "This job you can't stand."

How did he know?

"How would you feel at the end of it all? Looking back?" Tom is staring at me intently.

I know the answer, instantly.

"Like I wasted my life," I say.

Tom stamps on the last of the smoking embers with his boot.

"Well," Tom says. "Where I'm from, son, that's called a hell of a risk."

—

We ride in silence back to the house. It's not an awkward silence. It's just silence. I listen to the chug of the Ford, the birds, and the wind.

But in my mind, all I hear is the hum of bees. *A hell of a risk,* Tom had said. Was it true? Was I stuck in the honey trap? Too fogged up to leave? Too attached to the honey? By the time we reach the main house, my car is sitting in front of the garage. The rear tire is obviously new.

"Wow. That's some service," I say. "I thought I might have to hitch a ride to town."

"Earl added a car detailing business to his garage a while back," Tom says. "He was coming out here to pick up Alice's SUV anyway. Worked out just fine."

I look out at the view one more time. A bee buzzes past, then stops and begins to crawl on a flower near the edge of the driveway.

The honey trap, I think.

"I can't believe I just stood with all those thousands of bees," I say, "and I didn't get one sting."

"Honey can keep you docile, Noah. It's sticky stuff. Once you land in a pile of it, it takes a certain amount of effort to get out. A certain amount of courage."

The bee flits away, buzzing back in the direction of the hives. I watch the sun settling low in the sky.

"Speaking of income," I say. "I should probably get going and see if I can earn some. Thank you for your hospitality."

"Here, take this with you," Tom says, reaching behind the seat of the Ford. "A little souvenir."

He hands me a jar of honey. The label reads: TRIBUTARY ACRES HONEY.

I look up from the jar. Tom is watching me, a kind of knowing half-smile on his face.

"In my experience," Tom says, "as long as you get it from the right place, honey has a way of making everything a little better."

—

A few minutes later I'm on the road. The buzzing of the bees is gone, but I can't stop thinking about the honey trap.

I call Emma and tell her I'm on my way.

"What's going on?" she asks.

"What do you mean?"

"I don't know. You just sound different," she says.

I look at the fields flashing by on my left, watch the sun burning low in a blanket of clouds. I *feel* different.

I tell Emma I love her. That I'll see her soon. And for the rest of the drive, I think about nothing but bees and honey and the fog of life. I wonder if I really *could* do something different.

I remember Tom's words about spending the rest of my life in this job—in this honey trap: "How would you feel, looking back?"

The words come out of my mouth, fast and loud, "Like I wasted my life."

Was it possible? I wondered. Could I escape the honey

trap? Could I finally, *finally*, be in control? I stare down the road. It's a long drive home.

I start composing another resignation letter in my head.

3

REALITY CHECK

I wake up feeling just like Emma said . . . *different*. Part of the feeling is one that I recognize. It's the vaguely hungover feeling you get when you don't sleep enough. I feel just a little strung out, but alert at the same time.

The other feeling, though, is new. Usually, my first thought when the alarm goes off is some variation of *why me?* This is different. Is it the absence of dread? Is that the same as excitement? I'm not sure what to call it, but I think I like it.

Emma and I stayed up until the wee hours the night before. I'd recounted, as best I could, my whole experience with the beekeeper: the house, the estate, the bees, the works.

"I just feel like he *knew* me. Us. How trapped we feel."

Emma was supportive but cautious. "Did he say how to escape this 'honey trap?'" she asked.

"No," I admitted. "He talked about having streams of income, but he didn't really tell me anything."

Not long after that, I'd fallen asleep thinking about honey and streams and bees. Now, as I sit up in bed, I realize just how much my job has been draining our life together. I look over at Emma, who's still sound asleep. We both want kids, but we keep putting it off. The reason? Mostly my unreliable, unrewarding job.

"Next year," I keep saying, "things will be stable. We'll have some money set aside."

Next year always comes, but it's always the same story. I think back to what Tom said. *Honey is sticky stuff.* I slip quietly out of bed. *Things are going to change.*

I don't know how. But they're going to. They *have* to.

—

But they don't. I should know by now that things *never* change. The good feeling I woke up with—the one I carried with me through the shower and into the car and all the way to the office—vanishes within minutes of finding my desk.

My manager, Duncan, the guy with the account executive title that should be mine, appears almost instantly. It's like he's been waiting for me to show.

"I hear you had some car trouble," Duncan says.

"Yes. I sent in the expenses last night."

"Right. Yeah," he says. "Look, Noah. We had some changes come through while you were gone. Turns out that the car stipend we've been giving you—well, that's a taxable benefit, they say."

"What?" I ask. "I'm a full-time salesman. It's not a taxable benefit. It's . . . it's like a tool to do my job. Like a carpenter's hammer."

"Hey, *buddy*," he says with a cheeseball smile.

I grit my teeth. *Buddy*.

"I'm just as pissed as you are," Duncan says. "That's why we're changing things. We don't want you getting taxed more than you have to. So the car allowance is being changed. Now you'll get to write your *own* expenses off against your sales income. It'll be like a deduction."

He says this like he's just given me a Christmas present, and for a moment, I'm almost grateful. *Maybe they're finally doing me a solid*, I think.

Then I do the math.

"Wait a minute," I say. "That . . . that means I pay *every-thing* for my car. I'm on the road a *lot*."

"True, but you'll get to write it all off now," Duncan replies.

"But that's not the same as you actually *paying* for it!"

Now I'm truly pissed. Mr. Account Executive, however, doesn't seem to notice.

"Noah, *pal*," Duncan wheedles. "Do the math. This is a great thing for you. Besides, who wants to be on the wrong side of the IRS? No one *I* know, am I right?"

I'm speechless.

"Exactly," he says. Just as quickly as he appeared, he vanishes, like some nasty virus.

I sit in my stupid cubicle. I stare at the stupid fabric walls. Emma's face stares back at me from a photo of our honeymoon. Just the two of us. Not three. Not four. Two. No kids. No family. No future. No *control*.

The coarse walls of my cubicle stare back at me like the walls of a cell. *I need to get out of here. I need to get free. I need to get out of this honey trap.* I think of the mortgage payment and the car allowance I no longer have. I prop my elbows on the desk and slowly lower my head into my hands. *I'm never going to get out of here.*

I stay that way for several moments. Finally, I open my eyes and stare vacantly at the floor. My briefcase sits at my feet, tucked neatly under the desk.

My eyes focus.

The honey trap.

I grab the case, set it on my desk and pop the clasps. Inside is the tiny jar of Tributary Acres honey. I spin it around in my hands, almost frantic. Phone number. Where's the phone number? Why isn't there a damn phone number? I set the jar on my desk with an angry *thunk*. I stare at the walls. I stare at the honey.

Finally, I sigh and reach for the jar again. Maybe a little sugar will get me started on some calls. Car allowance or not, there's a mortgage to pay. I'll make a cup of tea, and load it with honey—like a morning kick-start—and then start working the phone.

I spin off the lid and look inside. Clear, golden honey. I dip a finger in and take a taste. It's good. Really good. Then I think about the honey trap, and the taste turns somehow bitter. I'm about to close the jar when I notice printing on the underside of the lid:

THE BEEKEEPER'S LESSONS

Lesson 1: Escape the Honey Trap
Transactions don't create wealth, equity does

I stare at the words. *Escape the honey trap.* That makes sense. But the rest? I'm not sure. Beneath the message in bold, black letters is a phone number.

I think back to my day with Tom. *I was so excited.* Now, the day seems like it was last year. Like it happened to someone else. *Someone else who isn't stuck in the honey trap*, I think.

I sit there, staring at the message on the lid. I remember what Tom told me. It all made perfect sense: the smoke, the honey, and the stickiness of our lives. But I just can't see *how* to escape. I don't have any money. I don't have any experience. I don't have any *time*. I don't know anything about the streams of income Tom spoke about.

I'll never escape the honey trap.

But I can't stop staring at the lid of the jar. It's like

the world around me has crawled to a stop. It's just me and a jar of honey. A jar of honey with a lesson that I just can't put to use.

Then it hits me: *Lesson 1.* One. As in the *first* one. As in the first of many? If there's a one, there must be a two, right? And maybe lesson two can teach me something else. Maybe lesson two can teach me how to break free.

Escape the honey trap.

I pick up the phone on my desk and punch in the number on the lid. It rings a few times before I hear the familiar, raspy older voice of the beekeeper.

"Hello."

"Tom? It's Noah Mason, I was—"

"How's the honey?"

I pause. "It's got a little extra something in it."

I hear him chuckle. "What can I do for you, Noah?"

I stare down the hallway. I can see Duncan in his private office, his feet up on the desk. He's grinning, yapping on the phone.

"I was wondering . . . would you be up for a visit?"

—

Minutes later, I stand up, grab my jacket, and head down the hall.

"Hey," Duncan says as I walk past the door to his private office. "Where you headed, pal?"

I don't even answer. All I hear is the buzz of bees.

THE BEEKEEPER'S LESSONS

1. Escape the Honey Trap

Transactions don't create wealth, equity does

TIME FOR ACTION

Putting the Beekeeper's Principles to Work

Prepare to create your first stream:

- Create a budget

- Begin to save 10% of everything you earn

- Build a $1,000 emergency fund

- Build your three- to six-month surplus fund

- Create your personal financial statements

Learn More About Creating Multiple Streams of Revenue

- www.jakeandgino.com/honeybee

Invest in Yourself!

If you consider yourself a lifelong learner, download our suggested reading list at

www.jakeandgino.com/readinglist

WWW.JAKEANDGINO.COM/HONEYBEE

4

THE ESCAPE

For the first time, I drive for hours without composing resignation letters in my head. It's not that I don't still want to quit my job. I want to more than ever. But instead of entertaining constant thoughts of quitting, of stopping what I'm doing, I'm thinking of moving forward—of *starting* something.

I just don't know what that something is. Or how it could even be possible. Once again I'm caught, stuck between the carrot and the stick.

Stuck. I look down at the jar of honey on the seat beside me. *Tributary Acres.* I remember what Tom said about multiple streams of income. How most people only have one income stream, and how that income can become a prison. A honey trap, like it is for the bees. *The real winner,* Tom had said, *is the guy that owns the hives.*

It makes sense to me that multiple streams are better than one. That's good old don't-put-all-your-eggs-in-one-basket wisdom. I understand that being in control—owning the hives, instead of being the worker bee—is better, too. If I was in control, my bosses couldn't keep changing things on me. What I don't entirely understand is the lesson printed on the lid of the honey jar: *Transactions don't create wealth. Equity does.*

For that, I need the beekeeper.

—

I pull into Tom's long laneway, and even though I'm expecting it, the grounds and sweeping vistas take my breath away. I follow the lane around to the garage at the back of the house, and I see Tom loading the old Ford with what looks like a big silver beer keg. He grins and gives me a wave.

"Planning a party?" I joke as I step out of my car.

"Not the kind you're thinking of," he says.

"I was hoping to ask you a few more questions about multiple streams of income," I say.

Tom hands me a bee suit. "I thought you might," he says,

"which is why we've got the honey extractor." He pats the big steel drum. "It's harvest time. Figured you might want to join me."

—

A few minutes later, I'm in my bee suit and we're chugging along in the Ford, headed for the old barn and the hives in the clearing beyond. A jar of honey sits between us on the Ford's wide bench seat. I pick it up and spin it in my hands.

"What did you mean by 'transactions don't create wealth, equity does'?" I ask.

Tom shifts the Ford into a higher gear. "You're in sales," he says. "So tell me, how do you make your money?"

"I sell products and I get a commission," I reply.

Tom nods, his eyes on the road. "Each of those sales," he says, "is a transaction. As long as you make that transaction happen, you get paid a little. That's your one stream."

"You're right about the 'little' part," I say. "My commissions have been shrinking."

"Well, here's the thing," Tom says. "The problem isn't the size of your stream."

I mull this over. "I don't know," I say. "It sure feels like that's the problem."

Tom pulls the Ford to a stop in front of the old barn.

"It's not that size doesn't matter," he says, stepping out of the truck. "It's just that two things matter *more*: the *number* of streams you have, and their *source*."

"I know I only have one stream," I say. "I can see how that's a problem. But what do you mean by source?"

"Your one source of income flows from transactions that you make. That means the stream doesn't flow unless *you* make the transactions happen."

"True," I say.

"The owners of your company, on the other hand," Tom says, "they get paid every time that you do—*without making the transaction happen*. That's because they *own* something. The source of their income comes from *equity*, from the ownership of value."

I ponder this as I follow Tom to the back of the truck.

"Like you own the hives!" I say, suddenly understanding.

"Exactly. I have *equity* in those hives. I own them. I spent the time and money to build them. But I did that once. Now the bees are doing the transactions all day every day. I just swoop in once in a while," Tom reaches up, pulls the steel canister from the back of the Ford and hands it to me, "and I grab the honey."

—

We put on our bee hats, and Tom leads the way to the hives in the clearing behind the barn. Once we're there, I set the drum down, and Tom motions for me to join him at the nearest hive. He bends down on one knee.

"See how each hive is actually a stack of separate boxes?" he says. "The bottom one is the actual hive. The others are called 'supers'. Yesterday, I put a board like this between the hive and the supers," Tom holds up a rectangular plank with a triangular device mounted on it. "It's called a bee escape."

"At night, when the temperature cools off, the bees all gather in the lowest box to stay warm," he explains. "But the bee escape only lets them go one way. It lets them escape the supers, but not easily get back in. Now, you and I can safely remove the upper boxes and harvest the honey."

Tom opens up the lid on the top box, and I see that, unlike last time, there are almost no bees inside—just row after row of vertical boards. He levers one of the boards loose with a putty knife and pulls it free. As he lifts it, I can see the hundreds of little octagonal cells of a honeycomb.

"Wow. Is that actual honey?" I ask.

"You bet," Tom says.

He scrapes the putty knife along the comb, and holds it toward me. There's a layer of clear, sticky fluid on its edge, mixed with bits of white beeswax. I lift up the front of my bee hood, and give the honey a tentative taste. It's pure, delicious, sugary *wonder*.

"Amazing," I tell Tom. "I can't believe bees make this."

"I couldn't agree more," Tom says. "It's amazing what hard work can do."

For the next couple of hours, we go through the process of harvesting the honey. We pull the combs from the hives a few at a time, and put them in the top of the steel drum. The drum has a handle, and with Tom's instruction, I learn to spin the combs inside, forcing the honey to leave the combs and drip into the bottom of the drum.

From there, Tom can turn the spigot on the outside of the drum, and drain the honey into buckets. After we harvest a few hives this way, something occurs to me.

"Didn't you say that honey is food for the bees? It's like money is to us," I say. "Something they need to survive."

"Yep," he replies.

"So, what will the bees eat?" I ask. "We took all their food."

"Ah. Great question," Tom says. "Just like you and me, the bees do need a certain amount to survive. There's a reason the upper boxes of the hive are called 'supers.' It's because they're *superlative*. That's just a fancy word for extra. A surplus, you might say. The honey you and I just harvested is their surplus honey. The bees don't need it to get through the winter. We've left them a good stockpile in the hive itself."

"So that's the honey you can take and use for other things," I say.

"Exactly. That honey gets packaged and sold, and is a nice little stream for Alice and I," Tom explains. "It's not a big one, more of a hobby, but we set it aside for a nice winter vacation every year."

Tom lets me know when the drum has enough honey in it, and we transfer it into larger buckets, which he says will then be strained and packaged properly for sale. We load the buckets in the truck and make our way slowly back to the house. I try to process the lesson in today's harvest.

"I think I understand the transactions versus equity thing now," I say. "You own the hives, you have the equity. You own an asset. The bees do the transactions—they work even when you're not around."

"Exactly," Tom responds. "That frees me up to do other things, but the stream of income keeps flowing."

"So the bees are in the honey trap, but you've escaped," I tell him. "What I don't understand is how *I* can escape. *I'm* in the hive. I'm deep in the honey trap."

Tom ponders this as we pull up to the garage.

"The secret to harvesting honey," he says, "is that you need a *surplus*. You need honey above and beyond the survival level. Without a surplus, all the honey would be used by the bees to stay alive."

"So I need a surplus?" I ask.

"Bingo. If you don't have any extra, anything to invest, it's hard to build equity," he says. "You're stuck in transaction land, with one unreliable stream."

I think of our monster mortgage payment. The car bills. The taxes.

"I'm pretty sure there's no surplus in my hive," I say. I mean it as a joke, but it doesn't sound very funny, even to me.

"Well, that may be," Tom says. "Luckily, though, you and I aren't bees. For us, surplus can take a few different forms."

"Like what?"

"Well, first there's money," he explains. "Surplus money can go to starting a business. Or investing in real estate, for example."

"What if you don't have any surplus money?"

"Well," Tom says. "One option is to create some."

"I think they call that counterfeiting," I joke.

Tom grins. "Yep. Frowned upon for sure." He grows serious again. "But before you give up on the idea of surplus cash, ask yourself whether you can either earn more or cut costs so that you have a little left over every month."

I think of the recent cancellation of my car allowance at work, and I'm not hopeful. "Are there other ways to create a surplus?"

"What you really want is a surplus that you can *invest*," Tom says. "And money isn't the only thing you can invest. If you have a few spare hours each day, that's surplus *time*. You could invest that in starting a business, for example."

I thought about our busy schedules. Did we have time? Maybe. It was possible, but we'd have to make some changes.

"Earl, the fella that fixed your car?" Tom continues. "He had an old barn on his property, much like mine. He emptied it, cleaned it up a little, and rented it out as storage space for boats and such. It wasn't much, but it got him a few hundred extra bucks a month. Enough to get him started on another second stream."

"So that was surplus . . . space?"

"Sure," he replies. "Anything that's an asset might be a surplus. Cash, time, assets like land, cars, and buildings—even skills and knowledge. They're all forms of equity that you can put to use. They're all surplus honey."

Tom starts to unload the truck. I look out over the rolling

green hills, across to where the small creeks merge to form the river that tumbles to the forest below.

I turn to find Tom watching me. "If you want to escape the honey trap, Noah," he says, "you need to find your surplus."

"I guess. I just can't see where we have any extra in our lives. I can't see how to get to this," I wave my arm, gesturing at his beautiful home, "from where I am."

"Every stream has its source," Tom says. "You just need to start. Sometimes the tiniest bit of extra is enough to get things rolling. Remember: It's not about the size of the stream."

I look back to the tiny streams merging into one river. "It's the number of streams, and their source," I say.

"Yep," Tom agrees and hands me a bucket of honey. "But for now, let's get this particular stream headed for the bank."

5

THE FIRST STREAM

I feel a strange mix of emotions on the way home. Tom's ideas are so simple, yet they feel *right* to me. It all makes sense.

My perspective on my job is shifting. It's clear now that I'm stuck in the honey trap. But while I used to think the solution was to get more honey out of the job, I realize now that the problem isn't the size of my income. The real issue is the fact that I'm relying on only one source of income, and that the source is transactional. It's not based on something I own and control.

Then I'm struck by something. All this trouble at work, the cutbacks, the commission changes, and the nonsense with my car allowance—in a way, they're a *gift*. If things were going well, I might never have been open to what Tom is teaching me. It almost makes me want to be nice to my manager Duncan.

Almost.

—

It's dusk when I pull into the driveway. I called Emma on the way home, and I know that she's inside waiting to talk about my visit with the beekeeper—or "Bee Man" as she's taken to calling him.

But I have one thing to do first. On the seat beside me is a jar of honey. It looks exactly like the last jar of Tributary Acres honey Tom gave me, but I have a feeling there's a subtle difference. I open the jar. Sure enough, there's writing on the underside of the lid.

- -

THE BEEKEEPER'S LESSONS

Lesson 2: Find Your Surplus

Every stream has a source

I screw the cap back on the jar. The porch light comes on, and I see Emma smile brightly and wave through the parted curtains of the front window. I feel a rush of affection, and, following it, a sense of something else. Something strong. Something like resolve.

- -

—

Over a long dinner, and perhaps a little bit too much wine, I tell Emma all about my visit with Tom—about escapes, and equity, and finding a surplus. The surplus idea intrigues Emma, but like me, she can't quite see how we can make it happen.

"What if we downsize our house?" she asks. "Try to simplify. Save more."

We talk it through. The truth is, it feels like a step back. We're planning a family, so if we downsize, we'll just be looking to upsize as soon as Emma gets pregnant. I know we can do it, but it doesn't feel right. Plus, I know from experience that moving isn't free. There are transaction costs, moving costs, and all the unexpected expenses of setting up a new place. In the end, I suspect it isn't really going to free up a lot of surplus.

Eventually, we shut down the idea, and I can tell Emma is relieved. We look at other options—maybe taking an extra job, or selling some of our stuff. Nothing seems to really resonate.

"Even if we could find the extra money," Emma says, "what do we do with it?"

"Honestly," I say, "I'm not sure."

"You could buy some hives from the Bee Man," she jokes.

"I think beekeeping is frowned upon in suburbia," I say.

She has a point, though. What *would* I do with the surplus? In the end, I decide that problem is a good one to have. The real issue is creating the surplus in the first place.

Every stream has a source. Where was mine?

—

Eventually, we run out of ideas and steam, so we head to bed. Emma climbs under the sheets and is almost instantly asleep. Me, I'm wide-awake and thinking about bees.

After nearly an hour of thinking and tossing and turning, I give up. I slip out of bed and pad quietly out of the room, closing the door behind me. I head to the spare bedroom, crawl under the covers, and try to get comfortable. At least here I can toss and turn without bothering Emma. Thank goodness for extra space.

My eyes snap open. Extra space. *Surplus space.*

I hop out of bed and head downstairs, turning on lights as I go. I make two stops in the kitchen: one to turn on a pot of coffee, the other to grab my phone from where it's charging. There will be no more sleeping for me tonight.

—

Two years earlier, we'd spent a fortune finishing the basement. Emma calls it my "man cave," but until this moment, I'd called it a stupid mistake. We had to borrow money to do the renovations, and it had just created one more monthly payment in a series that we could barely afford.

Now, standing there in the middle of the room, I'm seeing it in a new light. It's more than a basement, more than a monthly liability: It's something extra. A *surplus.*

Sure, we use the basement. But do we *need* it? No. Not if

it can become our first stream. The more I look around, the more I see how perfect it is. The basement is a walkout with its own entrance. There's a spare bedroom, a bathroom, and a bar with running water and a small bar fridge—plus the main TV area. All told, it's already practically a small apartment. Could it be that one of my biggest problems, a big house I can barely afford, might also be the answer I've been looking for?

I start walking through the place, tidying as I go. It's pretty neat already, but I straighten blankets and chairs, put things away, wipe down a few surfaces. Then I crank up the lights as far as they can go, and start taking photos with my phone. Next, I grab a pad of paper and a pen and start making lists.

—

By the time Emma wakes up, I feel like an entirely new person. I'm exhausted, but also exhilarated. The Beekeeper was right—the secret was in the surplus. I just had to find it.

When she comes downstairs to find me, I'm sitting in front of my laptop. On the screen is a photo of the very room we're in.

"Morning," she says, sleepily. "Whatcha doin'?"

"How would you feel about becoming landlords?" I ask.

She looks at the screen, then at me. "I think I'm going to need coffee for this conversation."

And with that, she turns and walks back upstairs.

—

An hour later, we sit side by side in front of my laptop. We're close; I can feel it. Not just the closeness of leaning into each other to see the screen, but the closeness of tackling something together, of sharing something important. There's a buzz in the air and it's not just the coffee.

On the screen now is a different picture of our basement. (Emma insisted on rearranging, tidying up herself, and retaking the photos. To her credit, they're a lot better.) Underneath the main photo is a description: *Cozy & Newly Renovated Private Suite.*

My finger hovers over the keyboard. One click and the profile goes live on a rental website. One click and we're in business. One click and—I hope—we've found the source of our first stream of income.

"Do it," Emma says. She's wide-awake now, bouncing on her chair. "Do it!"

I click.

—

Of course, nothing really happens. The profile goes live. We stare at it for a bit, as if willing something to magically change. Nothing does. We sit in silence.

"Breakfast?" Emma asks, at last.

"Sure," I say. "Breakfast."

I take one last look around my man cave. Or, our Newly Renovated Private Suite, which it is now. I feel a brief pang.

Is this the right thing? Then I think of the Beekeeper, Duncan my terrible manager, and our bills. I know that yes, this is the right thing.

Assuming it works, that is.

Emma makes waffles. I help, sort of. I'm distracted, and my head is miles away. I'm thinking about a stream of pure, clear honey dripping from a stainless spout. I'm thinking about our own stream—our *first* stream.

"Just leave it," Emma says, slapping my hand. "You're going to wreck the mix."

I stand back, hopping a bit from one foot to the other.

"No more coffee for you," she says, slapping a floury hand on the middle of my chest.

I flick flour in her face. She flicks back. I grab the syrup and threaten to pour it on her. Before things break out into a frat-house food fight, my phone buzzes.

"Truce! Truce!" I say, waving a dishtowel at her.

I pick up the phone and stare at the screen. My mouth falls open.

"What?" Emma asks.

"It's a booking," I say. "It's a *booking!*"

And just like that, we're in business.

THE BEEKEEPER'S LESSONS

1. Escape the Honey Trap
Transactions don't create wealth, equity does

2. Find Your Surplus
Every stream has a source

TIME FOR ACTION

Putting the Beekeeper's Principles to Work

- Your investment can come from any kind of surplus: time, money, or some other asset. What are your possible sources of surplus?

- Every dollar saved is a dollar you can use to buy assets that produce income. Can you start saving 10% or more of your income right now?

WWW.JAKEANDGINO.COM/HONEYBEE

6

THE STING

By the time fall arrives and the leaves change, something has changed for us, too: Our little basement enterprise has actually become a stream of income.

Both Emma and I are as surprised as we are delighted. Almost without fail, each weekend brings a new tenant for our rental suite. They are tourists, usually in town for a show or event, and our little spot is just close enough to be accessible to everything, but just far enough to be affordable. The income isn't much (as Emma says, I'm no Bee Man), but it's *there*. Our surplus space has transformed into a reasonably consistent trickle of cash.

The trickle isn't enough to quit my day job, to be sure, but something strange has happened in recent weeks. Even though the job hasn't changed, and my manager Duncan certainly hasn't changed—he's still a pompous, inauthentic *ass*—I just don't seem to care as much. The time I was spending writing resignation letters in my head and complaining about work is now spent watching the cash stack up in the account we opened especially for our rental income.

Emma is happier, too. In fact, we've been bragging to our friends a little about the easy money we're making as real estate magnates. "It's like an ATM," I'd told our neighbors. "It just keeps spitting out cash. We don't have to do anything."

As it happens, I'm at work telling a colleague about our 'easy, passive income' when Emma calls.

She asks, "Did you get the notification?"

"What notification?"

"This weekend's rental," she says. "They canceled."

"What? Why?" I ask, confused.

"A bad review," Emma answers.

I feel my heart sink. This is on me. I'm supposed to be taking care of all the communication online. Emma is in charge of the inventory of the basement. We take turns on the cleaning.

I vaguely remember getting a notification on my phone about a review, but we'd had a number of good ones, so I had stopped paying attention. Now, I pull it up on the screen of my laptop. *Damn.* There's more than one bad review.

"The previous tenant says the bathroom wasn't clean," I tell Emma.

There's silence on the line. *Uh oh.* "I guess it was my turn to clean," I say.

"Noah," Emma chides. "You can't just leave the place dirty!"

"I know, I know. I'm sorry." *How had I forgotten?* I'd just gotten busy, or maybe lazy. Maybe both.

I read the rest of the review. "They also say there were no filters for the coffee maker, and the ice maker in the fridge was broken."

This time it's Emma who's apologetic.

After we hang up, I post a response to the negative reviews, saying that all the problems have been resolved. But still, the damage is done. That's a lost weekend of income, and that review will be there permanently. There's no way to completely reverse the damage.

—

Luck seems to smile on us, however, and we get a last-minute booking through a different online rental portal. I confirm the booking, the tenants arrive on Friday as scheduled, and Emma and I quickly go back to congratulating ourselves on our stream of easy money. Then Sunday arrives.

I notice the tenants leaving by the 11 a.m. checkout, and I

think: *I should go downstairs and clean.* But, well, you know, it's Sunday. There's football—and naps.

The next thing I know it's almost dinnertime, and so I put off the job again. Finally, tired, and a little annoyed that I've waited so long, I trudge downstairs to clean up and check the supplies.

I can't believe what I'm seeing. The place is *trashed.* There are huge stains on the carpet. Red wine. *At least I hope it's red wine.* There are broken glasses, cracked plates, and in the air—is that cigarette smoke? And beer? The place smells like a frat house.

Then I see the blank spot on the wall: Our TV is gone. *Gone.* Where the flat screen once hung with pride, there are now only wires coming out of the wall. I'm still standing there, mouth agape, when Emma comes down the stairs behind me. Before she can say anything, I whip out my phone and log into the rental portal.

"*No!*" I hiss.

"What?"

"The deposit's already been given back."

"Call them," Emma says.

—

Thirty minutes later, I'm off the phone with the rental company. Not only is the damage deposit gone, but the people who rented from us have also closed their account and canceled the credit card. They've disappeared like ghosts.

"If you'd been a little faster to report the problem," the representative had said, "we could have sorted it all out."

I think back to my day spent watching football on the sofa. *Ouch.*

My call to the insurance company is no better. "You don't have a rider for rental use," their rep says. "I'm afraid this isn't covered by your policy."

I think back to our first booking. Changing our insurance was on the list of things to do. Now it was on the growing list of things I *hadn't* done.

I set the phone on the bar and hold my head in my hands.

"Don't worry," Emma says as we head to bed. "We'll sort it out."

But I'm seething. I'm angry at the people who mistreated us and stole from us, and angry at the rental company and the insurer.

I'm angrier still at myself.

—

The next morning, I'm still angry. And I'm feeling decidedly less smug about my 'easy, passive income.' I arrive at work a humbled man. The clean up of the basement and the replacement of the broken items eats two weekends of rental income. The TV is worse. It'll take three weekends to pay off the replacement, and the new one isn't anywhere near as nice as the one that was stolen.

The problem nags at me all day. It's not just the lost income, although that certainly sucks, but it's opened up a new set of questions: If we dropped the ball on this easy, tiny stream, what does that say about where we go from here? And where the heck *do* we go from here, anyway? Our supply of cash is building up in the rental account (minus a new TV and some repair costs), but what's next?

The truth is, having tenants in our basement every weekend isn't ideal either. The last time we had one of our own families over, they had to sleep on the living room floor. I *do* miss having my man cave.

I think back to Tom and his amazing home and property. How do I get from a basement rental, one that I can barely handle, to an epic estate? I can't connect the dots. I only have one basement. Even if I had more basements, I don't see how that gets me anywhere close to where Tom is.

The whole situation is leaving me feeling stuck, a feeling I know all too well. For the first time, I start thinking maybe it's the rental business I should be quitting, not this job. After all, the job is steady. It's predictable. No one trashes my desk while I'm away, or steals my computer monitor.

I look down the office hallway. Duncan is back in his usual spot, feet on the desk, talking on the phone. Blathering on without a care in the world. I feel a surge of frustration.

No. No way. I'm getting out of this place. I just need to figure out how.

I pick up the phone. *This,* I realize, *is a job for the Beekeeper.*

—

Though I haven't called him in months, Tom greets me on the phone like I was there yesterday.

"Of course," he says. "Come on over."

Minutes later I'm giving Duncan some bogus story about a new lead in the outskirts of my territory, and then I'm out the door and on the road.

—

If anything, Tom's estate is even more stunning than I remember. The fall colors are at their peak, and the view from his home at the top of the open field is a stunning riot of red, orange, and yellow leaves against the perfect green expanse of his lawn.

I step out of the car, and Tom is right there, bee suit in hand.

"Just in time," he says. "Got some hive repairs."

He hands me my bee suit. This time, I slip it on easily without help, and I'm ready in a jiffy.

"That was fast," he says.

"I'm a quick study," I joke.

With that, we jump in the old Ford and chug our way back in the direction of the hives. I give Tom a quick summary of the last few months. How we started our first stream. How easy it was. How the money was flowing in steadily.

He just nods and offers the occasional, "Mmm hmm."

We pull up behind the barn and step out of the truck. Tom grabs a toolbox and hands it to me, then disappears into the barn, and emerges a minute later with the bee smoker. A few moments later, we're smoking the hives.

Today's task is to repair a few of the frames—the thin boards that hold the honeycombs where the bees store their nectar. My job is to pry the sticky frames loose with a putty knife so Tom can repair them.

As I wiggle the frames free and pass them to Tom, I see something I didn't notice on our last trip. Each frame has a small brand on its edge, a logo of sorts burned into the wood. Some of the frames are pretty sticky, and it's hard to see clearly, but it looks like a circle with the letters "M I H" in the middle.

I'm about to ask Tom what the mark means when, without warning, a bolt of pain stabs into my wrist. It's as if someone has just jammed a hot poker into my forearm.

"Ow!" I yell, and jump up. I start flapping my arms and slapping at my wrist. It's like my arm is on *fire*. I yank up the sleeve of my suit, and a lifeless bee falls out. On my forearm, a welt is rising with a tiny red dot at its center.

I throw my glove on the ground in disgust.

"I got stung," I say, knowing I sound harsher than I should. I rub the swelling on my arm, which is getting bigger by the minute.

"What the hell?" I yell again. "Damn bees!"

I look up to find Tom watching me with what looks like sheer pleasure. He's not laughing, but he's close.

"What?" I ask, too aggressively.

That puts Tom over the edge. A snort escapes him first, then a chuckle, before he finally bursts into full, hearty laughter.

I feel the anger seep away and I smile. Just like that, I'm laughing along with him.

"Come on," he says, catching his breath. "Why don't we close up these hives, and you can tell me why you're *really* here."

7

THE ANTIDOTE

We retreat to the truck with the tools and frames and sit side by side on the tailgate. My outburst is behind me and the warm fall sun is on my face. I feel better already. My arm still aches, but I know it will pass.

"We had some issues with the rental this week," I tell Tom. I fill him in on the details. He nods and picks at some dirt on the metal edge of the Ford's box.

"So what's the problem?" he says.

"The problem is that *someone trashed our place and stole our TV*," I say, feeling the heat rise in my face again.

Tom is silent.

"Okay," I say, "The problem is that I didn't do what I was supposed to."

"Ah," he says. Then, after a moment, "You got stung."

"No kidding," I say, rubbing my arm. "Those little critters pack a punch."

Tom smiles. "I was talking about your business. Your first stream of income. You got stung."

"If that's what you call being robbed," I say, "then, yes. We got stung."

"Stings are painful moments," Tom says. "If you're trying to create streams of income, you're going to have more than your share of them. I've been stung plenty of times—by bees *and* by business."

There's a long silence as we stare out across the rolling hills of color in the distance.

"The thing about stings," Tom muses, "is that most of the time it isn't the bee's fault."

I look down at the angry red welt on my arm. "This is my fault?"

There's another long Tom-pause.

"Well," he says at last, "you got that bee suit on pretty quick when you arrived. Did you tuck your gloves inside the cuff like I showed you?"

I think back to how hurriedly I'd jumped into the suit. "No," I admit. Then I feel my cheeks burn as I think of how I'd bragged to Tom that I was a fast learner. "I was in a hurry to get to the hives. I skipped that part."

"Ah." Tom looks at the stack of frames. "Well. I know a bit about bees, and I know a bit about business. In my experience, I'd say most stings are a result of just that."

"Just *what?*" I ask.

"Being in so much hurry for the honey," Tom drawls, "that you forget about the work."

——

Tom gets off the tailgate and begins to hand me the wooden frames to load into the Ford. As usual, I realize, the old beekeeper is absolutely right. I hadn't checked on the apartment after the people left. In fact, the problems started even earlier, when Emma and I got complacent about doing the work necessary to keep things going.

It was even earlier than that, I realize. *It started the very first day you put off calling about changing the insurance.*

I think back to the bragging I'd done at the office about my 'easy money' and my 'ATM' and my 'passive income.' *What an idiot.* All that I'd really been doing was putting off the work of nurturing my stream. I feel my shoulders slump.

Tom hands me a stack of frames, and I catch another glimpse of that MIH brand.

"What's that mean?" I ask Tom, gesturing the best I can with my arms full.

"Ah." He stops digging through frames and stands up. "You might say it's my personal reminder of just what we've been talking about."

"How so?"

"MIH stands for 'Make It Happen,'" Tom explains. "It's a credo of sorts. A motto Alice and I thought up back in our early days, back when it felt like we were getting stung a lot."

"Make what happen?"

"Well," Tom says, "stings hurt, as you know."

I feel my arm throb. *I sure do.*

"But the most important thing about stings is that they have a way of scaring you off," Tom says. "You get stung once or twice, then you're reluctant to go to the hive. You get like the ostrich, burying your head in the sand. Avoiding the next sting, the next problem. The next thing you know, you're out of business."

"How does Make It Happen help?" I ask him.

"Well, it turns out the best antidote to a sting is to take action. To fix the problem," he responds. "Or better yet, to take action early and prevent the sting in the first place."

"Like I could have avoided my rental problems by being proactive."

"Yep," Tom confirms. "And that sting on your arm, too."

"So MIH reminds you to work hard and be proactive."

Tom squints his eyes, considering. "MIH is a reminder to work hard, like the bee. That helps safeguard your stream of honey, and it helps you avoid stings. When stings *happen*, MIH says to tackle the problems head-on by taking action."

"So I need to hustle, and not procrastinate," I say.

"Definitely," Tom says, "but Make It Happen is about more than just working harder. It's about *growing* harder. If you want your streams to multiply, you need to take risks. As a wise man once said, if you want to have more, you need to *become* more."

I think about Emma and our little suburban life, our paycheck jobs. "I don't know if we're the risk-taking type," I say.

"Maybe," Tom replies, "but, I like to think of the willingness to take risks as a skill, not a personality type. The courage to grow, to accept that you might get stung—that's not something you're born with. That's something you learn."

"How do I learn to not be afraid of stings?" I ask.

Tom chuckles. "Son, the bad news is that you get over your fear of stings by getting stung. No way around that."

"Oh." I look at Tom. "What's the good news?"

"The good news is that the stings are where the best honey is," Tom says.

"What do you mean?"

"The only way to get honey from the hive is to face the possibility of getting stung," he clarifies. "But the good news is that if it were easy, *everyone* would have beehives. Everyone would have multiple streams of income. Everyone would be wealthy. Stings are just nature's way of keeping the honey for folks who are willing to face a little risk."

I rub my arm; the welt is starting to itch. "But what if you don't want more stings? I mean, they're not that fun."

"No," Tom chuckles, "they aren't. But if you follow the MIH philosophy, you start to build up a tolerance to stings. It's like you develop antibodies to problems. The more you tackle problems head-on, the more you grow. The more you grow, the less the stings hurt." He raises his eyebrows and grins. "The more you grow, the more your streams of income grow, too."

We load the last of the frames and then sit back down on the Ford's tailgate.

"I've been thinking about streams," I say. "As in streams *plural*. We only have one right now, and it's not that big. Where do I go next? I only have one basement."

Tom cranes his head up, stares into the sky. I follow his gaze. At first, I see nothing, just small clouds moving across a stunning blue sky. Then I catch movement, and my focus shifts. I see a tiny shape dart across the sky. Then another. Then *dozens*. Maybe more.

"Bees?" I ask.

"Yep," he says. "Still hard at work. You'll see this all day when the weather's good. Takes tens of thousands of those trips to make a jar of honey."

"That's a lot of work," I say.

"Yep."

Tom stands up from the tailgate. "Nothing comes for free," he says. "People talk about passive income, but in reality, *passive* is a spectrum. Some things take a lot more energy, while others are relatively easy. But *everything* requires energy to keep it going. That's the MIH philosophy: If you want something, you need to make it happen. When you get stung, and stings happen, you have to move forward. The best antidote is action. You need to attack the problem head on, right then and there."

"So if I want to move to the next step in having more streams of income?" I ask.

"Get over your stings," Tom replies without missing a beat. "Make it happen. Lean into your problems and do the work."

"I get that, but . . ." I trail off. "I'm just not sure where to go from here."

"Well. I suppose a fella might ask himself a question," he says, then pauses.

I wait in silence while Tom ponders his next words.

"A fella might ask himself," he repeats, "if I can make one stream of income happen, why on earth can't I do it again?"

—

Five minutes, one handshake, and a jar of honey later, I'm on the road and headed for home.

I'm starting to see a pattern emerge with these visits. Every time I need help, I call Tom. He gives me help, and then I feel great. But after I leave, I find myself not quite sure how it is that he's helped me. It's a bit of a roller coaster.

Of course, with each visit there's the jar of honey. That's a pattern, too. I look to where it sits on the seat beside me, and then focus back on the road. *I'll look when I get home,* I tell myself. But my life has patterns, too, and they go back much further than my friendship with Tom. I know myself, and I *know* I'm not really going to wait until I get home.

Less than three minutes later I pull over on the side of

the road and spin the lid off the jar of pure, clean honey. As expected, the lid holds a message:

- -

THE BEEKEEPER'S LESSONS

Lesson 3: Make It Happen

Every source of honey comes with a few stings; the best antidote is action.

- -

THE BEEKEEPER'S LESSONS

- -

1. Escape the Honey Trap
Transactions don't create wealth, equity does

2. Find Your Surplus
Every stream has a source

3. Make It Happen
Every source of honey comes with a few stings; the best antidote is action.

TIME FOR ACTION

Putting the Beekeeper's Principles to Work

- Stings will happen. Adopt a "Make It Happen" attitude.

- When you feel paralyzed by a sting, write down the smallest possible next step you can take. It might be as small as looking up a phone number.

- Focus on taking action, no matter how seemingly insignificant. Even the smallest steps add up over time.

The Sting

- www.jakeandgino.com/honeybee

WWW.JAKEANDGINO.COM/HONEYBEE

8

THE SECOND STREAM

- -

"What if we charged more?" It's the next morning, and Emma and I are in the basement trying to digest the beekeeper's latest wisdom. Raising our prices is my newest idea.

Emma shakes her head at my suggestion. *Nope.*

"Okay," I try again. "What if we rent more often? Maybe during the week?"

Emma is silent for a moment. Then, without a word, she stands and marches upstairs.

"Hey! Where are you going?"

She returns a minute later with three jars of Tributary Acres honey, the ones Tom has been giving me. The first one is almost empty—it's not just Tom's advice we've been enjoying. I have to admit, the stuff is delicious, almost addictive. Emma sets the honey jars in a row along the bar top, and opens the first one. She lays the lid on the countertop, message facing up: *Transactions don't create wealth, equity does.*

"According to Bee Man—" she starts.

"Tom," I interject.

"Right, Tom," Emma says. "According to him, we needed to start thinking about *owning* things. Things that could generate money without us being tied to them all the time."

"Agreed."

"And then he told you this." Emma takes the lid of the second jar.

I read the message: *Every stream has a source.*

"He said the key was in the surplus," she says. "You find a surplus, and put it to work."

"Right," I respond. "That's what got me thinking about our basement—what started it all. So why not just charge a bit more, or rent more often? Then we'd have more cash coming in."

"Because," Emma says, "if we charge more, or rent more often, it's still money from the *same* stream. Bee Man's whole shtick is to have *multiple streams of income*, right?"

She's right. Boy, did I marry up.

"So," she says, "we need to take our *new* surplus—the cash

in our rental account from our first stream—and use it to create a *new* stream."

"Like what?"

"Well," Emma says, looking around the room, "what if we had more basements?"

—

Of course, Emma doesn't really mean more basements. She just means more rental space. She means for us to actually buy a rental *property*—a whole separate place.

"Think about it," she says. "Our place is always in demand. What if we bought another house? Where we could rent the upstairs as well. Maybe one with three or four rental suites! We'd have some real money coming in."

I start doing some mental math. She's right—four times what we're building up with our single basement stream feels like *real* money. Then I think of what's involved.

"It would take all our cash," I say, "and then some. Just to get the down payment together would be challenging." I rub the morning stubble on my chin. "I don't know. It feels risky."

Emma reaches out and takes the lid off the third jar of honey, and flips it over on the bar: *Every source of honey comes with a few stings; the best antidote is action.*

I look at the jar. I think of my visit with Tom. "That's the MIH philosophy," he'd said. "If you want something, you need to make it happen."

I look over at the wall, where a new TV hangs in place of

the missing one. I look at the carpet, once stained, now clean. *Those are all stings*, I think, *but they're behind you. You took action and got results. You took risks, and got rewards.*

I feel that sense of resolve sweep over me. I reach out and dip my pinky finger in the third honey jar, and hold it up.

"Deal," I say.

Emma grins, and dips her pinky in the jar, too. Then we link our sticky fingers together in a honey-glued pinky swear, and she gives me a kiss.

"Let's call our real estate agent," she says.

—

So we do. It doesn't happen fast, which is maybe a good thing, because I was freaking out just a little, but it happens.

Today is a crisp, sunny day in February. The colored leaves from my last visit with the beekeeper are long gone, but that doesn't stop my thoughts from wandering to Tom. Emma and I are standing on a street a few miles from our house. The sidewalks are lined with small banks of snow from yesterday's storm, and I hop from foot to foot, partly out of cold, but mostly out of excitement.

We're staring at a house. *Our* house. Not our suburban home, with its basement rental and the contents of our lives, but *another* house. This one is a triplex. It's got three rental apartments, and although they're empty, to me they're full of possibility.

It's taken some doing. We drained the account that had

been filling with cash from our basement rental, but we still had to get creative with the financing. It took some serious gumption and some hard work. A lot of it Tom would definitely call *Make It Happen* philosophy.

So here we are. Emma holds a set of keys in her hand—*our* keys, to *our* rental property. The deal closed today, and according to our math, which granted, is a little rough, after we pay the mortgage and taxes and the bills, and set aside a bit for maintenance, our little triplex will show a profit every month. This new house is going to *make* us money.

In other words, it's going to be another *stream.*

Emma jingles the keys, "Wanna go inside?"

I smile, and together we make our way through the slush, up the front walk, and into the next step of our lives.

9

THE BUSY BEE

It's 10 a.m., and I'm sitting in yet another pointless sales meeting. Outside, the rain falls in a steady drizzle. The sky is so dark that the city streets below are still lined with headlights, even at mid-morning.

Duncan stands at the front of the room, droning on while I inhale coffee like it's oxygen. I scribble on the pad in front of me. It looks like I'm taking notes, hanging on Duncan's every idiotic word, but what I'm really doing is the same math I've been doing for weeks, maybe months. It's the same math Emma has been doing, too.

The math is a simple equation that goes like this: If we buy one more rental property, I can probably quit this job.

The thought is intoxicating. I look to the front of the room where Duncan is writing some sales technique on the whiteboard. It's a technique he neither uses nor understands. I imagine standing up, walking past him and out the door while he calls after me, "Noah! Noah! This is a team meeting, pal!"

"Noah?"

I'm jerked out of my daydream by Duncan actually saying my name out loud. Maybe I don't look like I'm paying attention after all. I mumble an apology, and, satisfied, he goes back to talking.

I watch the rain, and the truth hits me fast and hard: *I'm still fantasizing about quitting.*

It's been more than a year since I met Tom. A lot has happened in that time—we added our first and second streams of income, and set aside a tidy bit of savings. But one thing *hasn't* changed, and that's how badly I want to leave this job.

The math tells me if we buy one more rental, I can.

Emma is on board. She's embraced the idea of multiple streams of income with every fiber of her being, it seems. She's never even met Tom, yet she's become the Bee Man's biggest fan. The problem is the workload.

The new rental property is going great. Like the basement rental, it's exceeding our expectations. But, as Tom said, nothing is truly passive. We're working for that money. While we used to spend our Sundays with friends or relaxing, we're now at the rental, cutting grass, doing minor maintenance. During the week there are calls from tenants, and rent checks to cash and bills to pay. There are contractors to organize for bigger jobs. That's all if nothing goes wrong.

When things *do* go wrong, it's like last week during the thaw. There was an ice dam on the roof. I got a call in the middle of the night from a renter who was woken up by actual drops of water hitting her face while she was lying in bed. That was a sting, to be sure. Thankfully, Tom taught me well. We're putting the MIH philosophy to work and taking action. We're tackling problems head-on, and getting things done, even when the inevitable stings happen.

Still, it's taking a toll. Most days, Emma and I are passing one another like ships in the night. At times we're a bit short with each other. I've certainly put on a little weight in the past six or eight months; I can't remember the last time I went for a run or hit the gym.

In short, multiple streams of income are starting to feel like multiple streams of *work*. It's a lot of time and a lot of effort. As Emma is quick to point out, though, it's a lot of *money*, too. Our rental account, which used to inch up each weekend from our basement bookings, is now climbing fast. Even with repairs and other expenses, the triplex is exceeding our expectations. So when Emma says she wants to buy another one, maybe even a four-unit, I can understand why.

What I don't understand is *how* we can do it. It would mean double the workload, and I don't see how we can possibly handle it. Yet, I *want* to be able to handle it. Like Emma, I'm doing the math, and the math is clear. If we can grow a little more, add another stream, maybe two, we can get *out*.

That's the idea running through my head as I sit through this pointless, gray Monday morning sales meeting: *We can get out*. I'm just not sure that we can survive the exit.

—

Finally, *finally*, the meeting ends. As I leave the room, I feel my spirits lift and my mind expand. *Maybe we could do it*, I think. We could get more organized. Be super-efficient.

Even still, I can't help but wonder: *To what end?* After all, even if we can handle one more place, I'm facing the exact same problem I was struggling with when I last visited the beekeeper all those months ago. I *still* can't connect the dots between where we are and the level of wealth that Tom has achieved. Sure, we might be able to work twice as hard. But there's no way we can work 10, or maybe even *100* times harder.

That voice in my head keeps saying, *what's the point?* If adding another stream means adding another pile of work, *then what is the point of all of it?*

I don't have an answer. But as I stare at the walls of my cubicle, I realize that I know someone who does.

—

In a last-minute flash of brilliance, I call Emma, who jumps at the chance to tag along.

"Promise me you won't call him Bee Man," I plead.

"Cross my heart," she promises.

The further we drive, the more we leave the rain behind, and the time seems to fly by. We chat amiably, and I realize that it's been a while since we've spent this much time together. As much as I'm enjoying it now, the thought makes me a little sad. More than ever, it's clear that our streams of income are coming at a cost.

An hour or so later, we pull up Tom's beautiful laneway. This time, I'm so entranced watching Emma that I'm not really even looking at the beautiful estate. She seems as mesmerized as I was on my first trip here.

"This is incredible," she whispers. "Look!" she exclaims, pointing at the deer grazing by the pond, just below where multiple streams converge into a small river.

Tom and Alice emerge from the house as we pull up. I barely manage to introduce Emma to Tom before she squeals, "Bee Man!" and practically jumps into his arms. I smile apologetically, but Tom is clearly delighted, as is Alice, and I feel the warm glow of connections well made.

Alice takes Emma on a tour of their unique house, something I know I'll never hear the end of. While they're gone, Tom and I lean on the old Ford, soaking up early summer sunshine while I fill him in on the events of the last six months or so.

Tom, always quick to listen and slow to speak, absorbs it all thoughtfully. Moments later, Alice and Emma emerge from the house, happily chatting. Alice carries a large wicker basket, the handle slung over one arm.

"All aboard," Tom says. We all squeeze happily onto the bench seat of the Ford. Tom starts up the old engine, and away we go.

A few minutes later, we near the barn. Instead of slowing down, Tom drives past.

"What about the bees?" I ask. "I was—well, *we* were—hoping to see them." *Hoping to learn another lesson*, is what I'm too shy to say aloud.

Tom seems to read my mind.

"Don't worry, son," he says. "There's more than one kind of bee in the world, and they all have lessons to teach us."

I look over at Emma, who shrugs and grins. From the corner of my eye I catch Tom give Alice a conspiratorial wink.

—

We chug along in the Ford, following the winding dirt road that passes the barn. I'm now in uncharted territory, and it occurs to me that this is how it always is with Tom—testing the unknown, pushing the envelope of what I know and what I *believe*.

The road dives back into a forested area for a short stint before we emerge into bright sunlight at the edge of a rolling meadow that stretches into the distance like vast carpet.

"Wow," Emma says. "It's beautiful."

She's right. The meadow is like a painting—lush green dotted with thousands of flowers in colors that seem to span the visible spectrum.

"You picked a beautiful time of year," Alice says. "The wildflowers are at their peak."

We clamber out of the front seat, and I take a deep breath of fresh country air, lightly scented with the sweet smell of blossoms. Alice leads the way to a small rise in the distance, sharing the load of the picnic basket with Emma. Tom and I bring up the rear, carrying blankets.

The rise is an even prettier spot, just high enough ground to still be dry, with a beautiful soft bed of wild grass to sit on. We spread blankets, settle ourselves down, and Tom begins to unpack the basket.

Our hosts have prepared something closer to a banquet than a picnic, and we munch happily. Emma shares some of our journey over the last year with Alice, and we all laugh at the image of Emma pouring over the lessons of the mysterious "Bee Man"—all the while eating a not-insignificant amount of honey.

At one point, Tom nods his head over my shoulder. I turn to look, and see a bee clambering over the purple crown of a flower.

"Do you think it's one of yours?" Emma asks.

I look at the bee, and I can tell almost right away that it's different. "It's longer. A different color," I say.

"Right," Tom says. "Good eye. Our bees are all honeybees, Emma."

She asks, "Where does this one live?"

"That's what's called a solitary bee," Tom says.

"You mean he's alone?" I ask.

"Other than for mating, most solitary bees are alone," he confirms. "They might live near other bees, but they don't live in social colonies like our honeybees."

I watch as the solitary bee lifts off and heads to another purple flower.

"That would make it hard to harvest honey," Emma jokes. "You'd have to find every bee home and take a tiny drop!"

"Actually," Tom says, "There are only a few species of bees that make honey, and solitary bees like this fella don't make any at all."

"Why not?" Emma asks.

"Honey comes from hives. And solitary bees don't have hives. They have small nests," Tom explains. "They don't live long, so they don't need to store food like honeybees. Even if they wanted to, they don't have the resources."

"What do you mean by resources?" I ask.

"Honeybees are social," Tom says. "Living in a community allows them to specialize, which means different bees do different jobs. Without that, they'd never be able to manage a big hive and create surplus honey."

"Poor guy," Emma says.

"In a way, yes," Tom agrees. "That fella, he's doing *all* the work. He doesn't live long, and he doesn't make honey. He's just struggling to get it all done by himself."

We watch the bee in silence, the warm sun on our faces. It's Emma who makes the leap, and she kicks me in the shin.

"Ow," I complain.

"That's us!" she says, her eyes lighting up.

"What?" I ask, not following.

"We're like the solitary bee!" she exclaims. "We're just struggling to get it all done by ourselves."

I see Alice give Tom a knowing look.

"Well, we have each other," I say.

"But we don't have a *hive*," she continues. Emma pats Tom on the knee, "and that means we can't make *real* honey!"

She raises her hands in triumph. Alice and Tom burst out laughing, and I break into a slow grin as I realize first that she's right, and then exactly just how dumb and lucky one guy can be all at once.

———

Emma's insight turns the conversation from bees to our struggles with the rental workload, and that seems to mark the end of lunch.

As we pack up the basket and fold the blankets, Tom explains that the vast majority of bees are solitary. Species of bees that work together, specialize, and create a lot of honey are actually quite rare.

"Like people," Alice adds, closing the lid of the basket.

It makes sense. Though as we drive back in the old Ford, I'm still wrestling with the problem we came here with.

"If we buy another place," I say, "we're going to be buried in work. I just don't see how we can do it."

"That's your problem, right there," Tom says, navigating the pickup through the woods.

"I know," I agree. "That's what I'm saying."

"No," Tom says, "I mean, what you're saying *is* the problem. You don't see how *you* can do it."

I look at Emma, and then back to Tom. "I'm sorry, am I missing something?"

Tom chuckles. "I'm messing with you a little. But the truth is there. The fact is, you *can't* do it."

I knew it, I think. I feel my shoulders sag a little.

"Because," Tom continues, "you're asking the wrong question. Instead of asking *how* you can do the work, you need to start asking *who* can do it."

"*That* will tell us how we can add another stream of income?" I'm skeptical.

"There it is again," Tom smiles. "That word: *how*."

Damn. He was right.

"Let me rephrase." I take time to choose my words carefully. "I keep thinking, *I don't see how we can do the extra work.*"

"Right," Tom agrees. "So just swap out the words. It's that simple. Ditch the *how*."

"I don't see . . ." I fumble for the right phrasing. "*Who* can do the work?"

Alice claps her hands. "Bingo!" she cries.

"Now," Tom says, "you have a question you can answer. *Who* can do the work that needs to be done if you buy another rental property?"

Emma speaks up. "I know this one," she says. "They have companies for that—property management companies. You can pay them to do that kind of stuff."

Tom says nothing. Just smiles and pulls the Ford up beside the house.

—

We leave in high spirits. It's been a lovely day, and I can tell that Emma is excited not just by the time we've spent together, but also by the lesson that Tom and Alice have taught us.

Alice gives us tight hugs. "You two remind me of us *so* much," she says.

Emma laughs. "If you saw where we live, you might reconsider."

"Oh gosh," Alice smiles. "You should have seen where Tom and I started!"

Tom grins. "Calling that place a shack would have been generous."

"Are you serious?" I ask, feeling skeptical again.

"We come from very modest beginnings," Alice says. "We had some good fortune, and we worked hard, but it was learning the principles of multiple streams of income that made the difference."

"Thank you," Emma says, giving Tom a hug, "for sharing them with us."

"Well," Tom says, "to give credit where it's due, it was

Alice who started putting the messages in the honey jars." He puts an arm around her affectionately. "She's the real brains of this hive."

"I can relate to that," I say, and I see Emma flush with pride.

Alice opens the lid of the picnic basket and hands a jar of honey to Emma.

"Just remember, Noah," Tom says, "you can't do it all. No one can. Wealth is a team sport—or, as I like to think of it, a *hive* sport. If you want a lot of honey, you need a hive."

"I think I understand that now," I say. "I realize I can't do it all. But if we pay someone, we'll be giving up that income. A property management company will take a lot of our profits."

"You'll be giving up *some* of that income," Tom says. "But you'll still keep some, too. More importantly, you'll be trading that income for something far more valuable."

"What's that?"

"The ability to add as many streams as you want," he responds.

"How so?"

"You need to start thinking of your streams of income differently," Tom says. "You're still in an *employee* mindset. You've found some surplus in your life and you've turned that surplus into assets, but you're still doing the transactions yourself. You're like solitary bees, doing everything."

"How should we be looking at our streams differently?" I ask.

"The lesson is in the hive," Tom explains. "You need to

make the leap from solitary bee to colony bee. You need to start seeing your streams of income as *businesses*. Once you add more people, that's what you'll get. Right now you own a job. When you build a hive, you create a *business*. A business is how you can create a *life*."

—

We climb in the car, and I can tell without even looking over that Emma is beaming, shining with excitement, and clutching the jar of honey in her hands.

We're only on the road for a few seconds before she's spinning the top off and looking under the lid. She reads the message aloud to me:

- -

THE BEEKEEPER'S LESSONS

Lesson 4: Build Your Hive
Learn to ask 'who' instead of 'how'

"Let me guess," I say with a grin. "It's time to call the real estate agent."

She doesn't reply. Just places the lid back on the honey jar, and then reaches over to hold my hand, where it stays for the entire drive home.

- -

THE BEEKEEPER'S LESSONS

1. Escape the Honey Trap
Transactions don't create wealth, equity does

2. Find Your Surplus
Every stream has a source

3. Make It Happen
Every source of honey comes with a few stings; the best antidote is action.

4. Build Your Hive
Learn to ask 'who' instead of 'how'

TIME FOR ACTION

Putting the Beekeeper's Principles to Work

- If you outsourced every task in your business to someone else, what roles would you need to fill?

- Write down those roles, and rank them in order of priority. Who do you need *first*?

- Start building your team! Remember: You don't need to hire full-time employees to build a team. You can use contractors and other service businesses.

- See Appendix B for a sample list of team members.

WWW.JAKEANDGINO.COM/HONEYBEE

10

THE THIRD STREAM

Just when you think things can't change any faster, they speed up.

I'm sitting in a window booth of my neighborhood café. It's early morning, and I've left Emma sleeping. I knew as soon as I opened my eyes that there was no going back to sleep for me.

This morning, however, I'm here for more than the coffee. I stare over the steaming mug in front of me, out the window and across the street to where two men are struggling to climb a pair of ladders while holding a huge sign.

The sign is wrapped in brown paper, but as they work their way up the ladders, a gust of wind tears the paper away, and I can see the words "Buster's Bistro." Something about how the logo is written jumps out at me, and for the first time, I notice the significance. The capital letters of each word are oversized. *Big b's,* I think. *Big bees.* I smile and take a sip of coffee. *How perfect.*

—

Buster's is more than a new restaurant in town. It's a new stream of income for Emma and me, and we're excited. It's been almost exactly a year since our last visit to the beekeeper, and what a year it's been.

Once we grasped the lesson of the hive and began to see our rental properties as *businesses,* everything shifted. Within days of arriving home, Emma had arranged housekeeping and maintenance companies to take care of almost all the weekly demands of the rental units—even our basement one!

That, in turn, freed us up to buy not just one more income property, but *two.* One we used for short-term rentals, like the others, and the other we rented to long-term tenants. At first, Emma was skeptical that we could afford the second place, but after a quick phone consultation with Tom, we arranged for the owner to finance the mortgage.

Our new "hive mentality" was paying off. In less than two months, we were now the owners of multiple properties and multiple streams of income. Best of all? I was no longer the owner of a sales job!

For all my fantasizing about quitting, the actual moment was nothing like I had imagined. Something had changed in me—once I had the freedom to leave, it was as if all the resentment I felt had drained away. I almost felt *sorry* for Duncan. I'd wished him well and walked away feeling nothing but contentment.

Now, here in the cafe on a beautiful spring morning, "Noah the sales guy" seems like someone else. It's been less than a year, but my corporate job feels like a boring page in a story about a stranger, a story about some other Noah, one who's trapped in a life he doesn't want.

This Noah, on the other hand, the Noah who's drinking coffee and watching the sign-makers across the road? He writes his *own* story.

———

Right now, the story is an exciting one. Within a year of purchasing the new properties, we were once again feeling pretty flush with cash. We weren't rich, and we certainly didn't have Bee Man levels of honey, as Emma would say, but things were changing, and they were changing fast.

Along the way, word had trickled out. We had money in the bank, and our friends and families certainly knew about our projects. So I wasn't entirely surprised when we were approached about making an investment.

It was a friend-of-a-friend type thing. The guy, *Buster* of the Buster's Bistro that was at this moment opening across the street, was a Cordon Bleu chef who'd come to town scouting locations for a restaurant he wanted to open. He got in touch and shared his business plan with us.

It took some time, but eventually Emma and I decided to invest. We had the cash, and we wanted to branch out. We wanted another stream. Besides, it was *exciting*.

"Just think," Emma had said. "We can go for dinner at a fancy French restaurant any time!"

"As long as you like your food with honey," I joked. But in truth, that was the most thrilling part: If everything went according to Buster's plan, there would be more than enough honey for everyone. From there, Buster had ambitions to open bistros in multiple cities. Of course, we would have the first refusal rights to partner on those restaurants, too. It was all very intoxicating.

Sipping my coffee and watching the sign appear over the freshly renovated restaurant, my excitement is only growing. *B's*, I think, staring at the two oversized letters on the sign. *Bees make honey.*

—

The invite-only opening of Buster's Bistro is a roaring success. Buster seems to have a flair for food and publicity, and the place is packed.

Emma and I weave our way through the pre-dinner cocktail crowd, feeling the glow of success and basking in the idea that *we own a restaurant*. Still, we try to keep a low profile, we're only silent partners, after all, but Buster introduces us to everyone as, "the best partners ever." The title is touching, and an ego-stroke to be sure. But for a brief moment I wonder, *how many partners have you had?*

The thought vanishes, however, as Emma grips my hand and gives me a kiss on the lips.

"This is so great!" she says.

She's right. It might be the wine, but this experience is a little intoxicating. We share a table for two, Buster's prime chef's table, and drink two bottles of very expensive wine, leaning our heads toward each other as we plot and dream of our growing hive and multiple streams of income.

—

It's Emma who notices the cracks in the metaphorical honey jar first.

For the first month or two after the opening of Buster's, we eat there a couple of times a week. We enjoy the privilege of fine dining with no reservations, little cost, and, I have to admit, a modest amount of attention. It's no secret that we're investors in the restaurant, and occasionally I catch a glimpse of diners nodding in our direction and whispering across their tables.

Inevitably, however, the novelty wears off. I can't help but notice that all the French food is not helping my expanding waistline. So, as the weeks pass, we go to Buster's less and less. In fact, we *talk* less and less to Buster himself. Things just seem to be moving along as they should.

"Our hive is making more honey," we tell ourselves.

One night, after a particularly long day managing more than a few stings from what had now become almost a dozen rental units, Emma comes through the door and flops on the couch.

"I can't even think of cooking," she says.

"I'm starving," I say. "Let's go to the Bistro. Besides, we haven't seen Buster in ages."

—

We park behind the restaurant, in the reserved space, of course. As I get out, I notice something different: The lot is half empty.

"Must be a game on," Emma says, looking around.

"Sure," I agree halfheartedly. Suddenly, I'm not as hungry as I was.

Inside, we're taken to our usual table, but the place is practically deserted. When the waiter comes to take our drink order, I ask him to tell Buster we're here.

"Oh," the waiter says matter-of-factly, "I doubt he'll be in."

He's right. Buster doesn't make an appearance.

Of course, that doesn't *mean* anything. Everyone's entitled to time off, naturally. There's nothing to worry about.

Despite my rationalizations, the wine—a wonderful vintage—leaves a sour taste in my mouth. I pull out my phone halfway through dinner and send Buster a message.

—

Buster doesn't reply. Not that night. Not the next day. He doesn't answer calls either.

After two nights with no response, Emma asks, "Do you think something happened to him?"

"I'm sure he's fine," I say, but inside me a voice is saying, *something is off.*

I drive by Buster's Bistro again that night. The parking lot is almost empty. Through the restaurant window, I can see the staff killing time aimlessly tidying empty tables. I don't sleep well.

—

I wait as patiently as I can, but by the fifth day, I'm beyond restless. The restaurant is clearly suffering. There are never more than a couple of cars in the lot. The staff confirms my worst fear: No one has seen Buster in weeks.

I wait until Emma is out of the house for a few hours, jump in the car, and drive to Buster's home. As I pull up, I'm half expecting to find he no longer lives here. That he is, in fact, some sort of con artist who's picked up and disappeared to a palm-studded Caribbean tax haven with all our cash. I picture him lying beside a pool, laughing loudly while waiters bring him blue-umbrella drinks and call him "Mister Buster."

My stomach sours, and I feel the anger rise. But Buster isn't gone, and he certainly isn't tanned. When he answers the door, Buster looks only pale, resigned, and unsurprised to see me. He simply opens the door and steps aside for me to enter.

—

It all ends with a whimper. There was no con, no scam—Buster simply messed up. He misjudged the market, and spent too much money on furnishings and renovations. A shocking amount of money, I realize, when I press him for the numbers. When I push further, it becomes clear that while Buster certainly has a track record for opening restaurants, it's a *lousy* track record. He's left a trail of disappointed investors and shuttered ventures in his wake.

The reality is simply this: The restaurant is a lost cause. Our money, all our hard-earned, painstakingly saved cash is lost along with it.

—

I'm sitting at the kitchen table when Emma comes home. I tell her about Buster.

She nods, seeming unsurprised, too.

"I'm so sorry," I say. "I should never have gotten us into this."

Emma says nothing, and instead walks across the kitchen and opens the cupboard. She returns and sets a box of crackers and a jar of honey on the table. We sit there, dipping crackers in honey and eating in silence.

"I can't believe this," I say. "It's terrible."

Emma chews thoughtfully.

"Well," she says, "it's not great. But I have an idea."

"What's that?" I say through a mouthful of crackers.

"Call Duncan tomorrow. I bet you can have your old job back in a heartbeat."

I nearly spit my crackers on the table. "Are you serious?" I ask her.

Emma grins. "Of course not, dummy. Look, this is a sting, and it's a bad one, but we still have our streams—and our dreams. Would you rather go back to your old job? To the way things were?"

I consider for a millisecond.

"No way," I say.

"Then here," she flicks the lid of the honey jar to me. I read it.

- -

THE BEEKEEPER'S LESSONS

Lesson 3: Make It Happen

Every source of honey comes with a few stings; the best antidote is action.

"How about we quit feeling sorry for ourselves," she says, patting my arm, "and call the Bee Man?"

- -

11

BEES OF A FEATHER

This time, I make the drive to the beekeeper alone. I need the time to think, and besides, Emma's working. The loss of the restaurant income was painful, but there are some unexpected costs in the rental business, too. Emma's taking on some of the property management duties just to shore up our cash flow. We were paying those guys a fortune, so it'll certainly help. Still, it's disappointing to be forced to take a step back.

I know it's more than just disappointment, though. It's as if the lost investment has tainted my view of everything.

Emma is calling it a sting, but it feels like more than that to me. To me, it's a *failure*, and I need to know why it happened.

Emma and I have gone over the situation a million times, dissecting the story like forensic technicians with a corpse. Yet, for all our analysis, I still don't truly understand where we went wrong. I understand what happened in hindsight, but what I can't sort out—and what I *need* to sort out—is how I can stop it from happening again.

How do I know our next investment won't do this? I need *foresight*, not hindsight. It's not so much that I need to be able to predict the future. I know that's impossible. I just need to predict *myself*. How do I know I won't make the same mistake again?

I rub my shoulder. Roll my head around. I'm stiff, stressed. The drive isn't helping this time. It doesn't feel like my visits to Tom. I've come to him with problems before, but this feels bigger somehow.

As if the weather is attuned to my thoughts, rain starts to spatter the windshield. Leaving the interstate on my way to Tom's, I say a tiny prayer in hopes that the beekeeper hasn't run out wisdom.

——

It's still spitting rain when I arrive, and Tom invites me inside. I sit at the bar to one side of his cavernous main living area, enjoying the view while Tom makes coffee. I discover it rivals anything a professional barista could brew—sweetened with just a bit of honey, of course.

"This is delicious," I say. I feel better already. Just being around Tom is somehow reassuring.

"I'm no restaurateur," Tom says, "but I do enjoy a good cup of coffee."

"Funny you should mention that," I say, and I tell him the story of Buster's Bistro, and how we discovered the place was slowly going under.

"I'm no restaurateur, either," I say, "but even I could tell there was no way that place was covering its costs."

"Exactly," Tom says.

I nod in confirmation.

"No, I mean you *aren't* a restaurateur," Tom says, startling me. I set my coffee cup down, feeling suddenly awkward.

"It's not just a figure of speech," he continues. "You really *aren't* a restaurateur. The economics of food is tricky. It takes more than a talented chef to make it work. You need to understand the market and its trends. You need to make tough choices about who is and who isn't your customer. Margins can be razor thin."

"I wish I'd known that a few months ago," I say, staring into the dregs of my coffee.

Tom looks out the enormous front windows of the room. I can tell he's trying to decide whether or not to say something.

"What?" I prompt him.

"Well," he says at last, "the thing is, you probably *could* have known."

He picks up my empty coffee cup and places it in the sink behind the bar.

"Follow me," he says. "I have something to show you."

—

Outside, Tom and I stand at the top of his rolling estate. I can see the last of the weather moving away to the east. It's damp out, but the rain itself seems to have passed.

Tom points down and to the right, where the series of small creeks and tributaries make their way downhill.

"When Alice and I first walked this property," Tom says, "it was all scrub and old orchard and some woods. We found these streams on the first visit with the realtor, and we took it as a sign. Might be silly, but that was all we needed to know that we'd found the right spot."

"I like the symbolism," I say, and Tom seems pleased.

"Notice anything about those streams?" he asks.

I look more closely. There are several of them, some seeming to come right out of the ground, like a spring. Others meander out from the woods. Whatever the source, I notice they tend to head toward one central stream that's a little larger than the rest.

"One stream is bigger," I say.

"Yep," Tom confirms.

I follow the flow of the main stream. As more and more tributaries join in, it grows, eventually swelling to become the river that lets out into the pond at the bottom of the clearing.

"Think of that bigger stream as your *core* business," Tom says. "All the streams have water, and they all flow downhill, but the smaller streams feed the larger one. They start separately, but at some point, in some way, they're all connected."

"I'm not sure I understand how that would have helped me avoid Buster," I say, knowing Tom's making a larger point I can't grasp yet.

"One of the most important rules of creating multiple streams of income," Tom says, "is to identify your *core stream*. That's your hive. It's your main business that creates the majority of your honey, at least for the moment."

"Let me guess," I say, chuckling. "The restaurant business isn't my core." *At least I'm finally laughing a little about this*, I think.

Tom chuckles along with me. "Let's take a drive."

———

When we reach the old Ford, I'm surprised that Tom tosses me the keys.

"Really?" I ask.

"At my age, it's nice to be chauffeured once in a while," he grins.

At his age? To my mind, Tom is ageless. He seems to have an unlimited supply of energy.

"What about the bee suits?" I ask.

"Not this time," Tom says. "Head the other way down the road. Toward the pond."

I climb behind the wheel. The inside of the truck is spartan, and it takes just a few seconds to familiarize myself. The engine turns over easily, and within moments settles into a steady purr.

I guide the Ford downhill, away from the old barn. To our right, I can see the various small streams tumbling down the slope, merging in pairs, then merging again, and finally meeting in the small river. Tom points to a flat spot near the pond. The ever-present herd of deer scampers into the woods as we pull up, their white tails flashing. We step out of the truck and walk to the edge of the water.

"So," I say, after the last deer disappears from view, "clearly the restaurant business was the wrong choice."

"Well, let's not throw out the honey with the beeswax," Tom says. "What you need to do is see things through the lens of your core business. Let's say this fella, this Buster, was coming to you now. Based on what you know, what would you say?"

I laugh, an abrupt bark that slips out before I can stop it.

"I'd throw him out the door!" I say.

Tom just shrugs, and I can sense his disagreement.

"Wouldn't *you*?" I ask, in astonishment. "I mean, the business failed."

Tom bends and picks up a stick from the edge of the pond. "You might be right," he says. "There may never have been an opportunity there. What I'm suggesting is that before you decide, you might look at it through the lens of your core business. Right now, that's real estate."

I take a deep breath, and try to forget about all the money I've lost on Buster's Bistro. "Okay," I say. "I'm not in the restaurant business. I'm in real estate. So, I simply say no."

"Yep. That's one option," Tom agrees. "Well considered. What else?"

What else?

Tom picks up on my confusion. He tosses the stick, a long, overhand throw that lands perfectly upstream in the main river. A moment later, the stick washes into the pond.

"Here's a hint," he says. "Buster's restaurant is a way for him to make honey, right? It's his business."

"True," I say. "It was a lousy one, mind you."

"Forget that," Tom dismisses the idea. "Think instead about what you know about making honey. What does every bee need?"

"A hive," I say, after a moment. "A place to make the honey."

"Right," Tom says. "You might not be in the restaurant business. But you sure *could* be in the business of renting real estate to restaurants. You could also be in the business of helping restaurants buy real estate. You could loan them money, for example. I'm not suggesting Buster would be a good bet, but the first way you analyze any opportunity should be through the lens of your core business."

"How do I do that?" I ask.

Tom picks up another stick, and this time he tosses it into one of the smaller tributaries.

"It means," he replies, "you ask yourself, *how does this connect to my main source?*"

We watch as the stick he threw bobs along the small stream, then pops into the main river.

"The best streams feed each other," Tom says. "That's how you get a river of income. Eventually," he points at the stick as it bobs into the pond, floating lazily, "that income builds into something significant."

"Why is it so important for streams to feed each other?" I ask. "I mean, there are probably some great opportunities out there that aren't related to real estate. I just picked a bad one."

"First of all," Tom says, "your core business is what you *know*. You get better at it all the time. Sticking to opportunities related to your core business means you're less likely to make mistakes. Your odds of success go up. It's like going into the casino with an edge."

I watch as the water continues to tumble into the pond. "I can see that," I say. "Part of the problem was that it was getting hard to find another good deal on a rental property. I wanted to put our surplus to work, just like you taught us, but I couldn't seem to do it."

"Believe me, I understand," Tom says. "When things are going well, when you have a surplus, opportunities have a way of becoming more appealing. They become shiny objects that catch your attention. Like a pretty flower might catch the eye of a bee. Your job is to analyze those shiny things, to bring the lens of your core business to them, and see if they *still* seem shiny. A bee can't make honey from every plant, even if it's pretty. They use a lot of different ones, but not *all* of them."

"So it's about resisting temptation?" I ask.

"That's part of it," Tom says. "Creating great streams of income is as much about saying 'no' as it is saying 'yes.' But there are benefits that come from having connected streams. When your streams are connected, you have a better chance of success, because your knowledge carries over from one stream to another."

"Right," I agree, "or doesn't, in the case of Buster's Bistro."

"Exactly," Tom says, "but there's more to it. Related streams can share common customers and common brands. That means it can be faster to grow a stream because you might already have a customer base ready. Like when an auto mechanic offers a car detailing service, they already have a base to sell to. Plus, related streams can share some common expenses or equipment. That means when you add a connected stream, it might be more profitable more quickly."

"That's a pretty compelling list," I say.

"Some folks call these advantages 'synergies,'" Tom says. "I just think that the best streams feed each other. They give you momentum."

In the distance I spy a deer, tentatively working its way back to the pond, keeping a watchful eye on us.

"I guess we shouldn't have picked the restaurant business," I say glumly.

"Perhaps," Tom says. "But there's another way to look at that, too. When you created your first stream, you started small. You were treading into a new area, so you started by renting out your basement. The stakes were low."

I had never thought about it, but it was true. Failing to rent our basement wouldn't have been that painful: Life would have just gone on as usual.

"It sounds to me like you put a fair bit of cash into that fella Buster's place," Tom says.

He's right about that. We lost a *lot*. We drained our savings and then some.

"Around here," Tom says, his drawl coming out strong, "folks say if you're going to bet the farm, you should know a lot about the weather."

I laugh at Tom's folksy knack for making failures seem a little more palatable, but I know he's right. We bet big on something we knew nothing about and got in way over our heads. We tried to do our due diligence, but there was no way we had the skill to accurately assess Buster's business plan.

"So I should make smaller bets?" I ask.

"When you're treading into unknown territory, I think small bets are a good way to test the waters. Or," he grins, "taste the honey, if you prefer."

We toss a few more sticks in the water, like little kids playing after a rainstorm, then walk back to the Ford.

"I'm still wondering where to go next," I say. "Finding rentals is tough right now, and we do want to keep growing."

This time Tom gets behind the wheel of the truck. "I can tell you," he says, starting up the engine, "some of my best streams came from watching which way things were flowing."

"What do you mean?" I ask.

"Streams flow both ways," Tom says. "Or, as the old saying goes, you have to spend money to make money. I've found that watching the money flowing *out* can be a great way to get money flowing *in*."

That seems to make no sense at all. I'm about to ask Tom about it, but he pulls the old pickup to a stop near the garage. He kills the engine and just sits there. Once again I'm struck by the thought that he has something to tell me.

"Everything okay?" I ask him.

He continues to stare out the windshield. "I was about your age when things really started to take off for me and Alice," he said.

"Well," I say, "I only hope things work out as well for us."

Tom smiled faintly. "The stuff I've been telling you over the years," he said, "it works, you know."

"Believe me, I know," I tell him. "Why do you think I keep coming back here?" I laugh, but Tom's barely smiling.

"I mean, it *works*. All those little streams, they start to build up. They start to pick up speed. They begin to flow together, and before long . . ." he trails off.

"Before long what?"

Tom turns to look at me. "Before long, you can have a hell of a river."

"That sounds pretty exciting to me," I say. "That's just what we're looking for."

Tom taps the steering wheel thoughtfully. Takes a breath, and lets it out slowly.

"Yep," he says at last. "I suppose it is."

"You know what?" He slaps the dash of the Ford with his hand and forces a grin on his face. "I almost forgot to give you your honey!"

He hands me a jar, and before I can even say thank you,

he's out of the truck. We say our goodbyes, and this time they seem almost hurried, as if Tom is feeling unsure. Moments later, I'm on the road.

As I drive, I keep thinking back to Tom's comment. What did he mean about a hell of a river? That sounds like exactly what we're looking for. Eventually, I give up trying to decipher Tom's message and decide he was just having a bad day.

When I stop for gas halfway home, I can't wait any longer. I open the jar of honey to find the beekeeper's latest lesson:

THE BEEKEEPER'S LESSONS

Lesson 5: Commit to Your Core
The best streams feed each other

I spend the rest of the drive deep in thought. I'm not sure if I completely understand what Tom has told me today, but once again, I'm *energized*. By the time I'm home, Tom's uncertainty is a fading memory.

THE BEEKEEPER'S LESSONS

1. Escape the Honey Trap
Transactions don't create wealth, equity does

2. Find Your Surplus
Every stream has a source

3. Make It Happen
Every source of honey comes with a few stings; the best antidote is action.

4. Build Your Hive
Learn to ask 'who' instead of 'how'

5: Commit to Your Core
The best streams feed each other

TIME FOR ACTION

Putting the Beekeeper's Principles to Work

- What's your core business?

- What possible streams of income can you imagine that are related?

- What other opportunities within your streams can you envision?

- Refer to Appendix A for suggestions and examples.

Creating Your Surpluses

- www.jakeandgino.com/honeybee

WWW.JAKEANDGINO.COM/HONEYBEE

12

THE RIVER

For the next few weeks, Emma and I find ourselves in crisis-management mode, and my visit to the beekeeper is all but forgotten. Cash flow is tight. The loss on Buster's Bistro was painful, but it also creates another problem we didn't count on: We have no reserves. All our cash was tied up in the restaurant deal, and now we find ourselves dipping into credit to keep the business running day-to-day. When that runs on too long, interest payments start to stack up, which tightens cash flow ever more. It's a slippery, dangerous slope.

The leaky roof at the rental property, the one that dripped water on the tenant in bed, turns out to need more than a simple repair. The water had been leaking for months, and when I climb into the attic to investigate a strange smell, I discover huge areas of the roof sheeting and structure are rotten, and there's mold in the ceiling. It's fixable, but expensive, and Emma and I are struggling to come up with the cash. It can't wait.

Our slippery slope is getting steeper.

—

It's early evening, and Emma and I sit side by side at the kitchen island. I've got my laptop open, and Emma has spread a flurry of quotes and bills and financial statements across the countertop.

"I talked to the bank today," Emma says. "We can borrow the money for the roof."

"But then we'll have loan payments to make," I say. "So, if anything, our cash flow problem will get worse."

"True," Emma says, glumly. "Plus, we can't buy another rental property with all this cash going out. We'll be treading water at best."

"No kidd—" I break off. Something in Emma's words has sent my mind in another direction.

I get up from the counter and begin opening kitchen cabinets.

"What?" Emma says.

"Where is it?" I ask absently.

"Where's *what?*" Emma responds.

I head to the spare bedroom that we've converted to an office, and rummage around.

"Noah?" I hear Emma from the other room.

Cash going out. I rummage through my desk. "There you are!" I say, triumphantly.

"*What?*" Emma asks again from the other room.

I walk back into the kitchen carrying an unopened jar of honey. "Tom gave me this on my last visit. With everything going on, I'd forgotten all about it."

I sit back at the counter and spin the lid off. The lesson from the beekeeper is neatly printed inside:

- -

THE BEEKEEPER'S LESSONS

Lesson 5: Commit to Your Core
The best streams feed each other

I realize that in all the chaos I had never even told Emma about my visit. I recount to her how Tom had done a kind of post-mortem on our experience with Buster. I explain how we need to focus first and foremost on streams of income that are related to our core business. We'd have to be wary of shiny objects, those investment opportunities that might be out of our depth, unrelated to our core.

"What's that got to do with the roof?" she asks.

"I asked Tom how we could find new streams," I explain. "He said something about how 'watching the money flowing out can be a great way to get money flowing in.'"

"What's that supposed to mean?" she asks.

"I'm not sure, to be honest," I admit. "I don't understand it myself. But he's never steered us wrong before."

Emma purses her lips in thought. She looks at the jar of honey, and then at the papers sprawled over the countertop. "Do you have our profit and loss statements for the last couple of quarters?"

"Actually," I say proudly, "*I do.*" After Tom had urged us to treat our streams of income as *businesses*, we had decided we should get proper bookkeeping.

"Better yet," I say with a flourish, "I have them right here on the screen."

I pull up the last couple of financial statements. Emma leans in and begins to scroll.

"What are you looking for?" I ask.

"Money flowing out," she says. "Isn't that what Bee Man said?"

I stare at the screen. "It seems like *everything* is money flowing out."

"True," she says. "But, still."

She scrolls further, occasionally backing up to check some figure on a previous screen.

"Look at this," she says. "Look at how much we're

paying for property management. The more properties we add, the higher it goes."

"Sure," I agree, "but that was deliberate. We needed to do that to free up time so we could grow. That was about asking *who* instead of *how*, remember? Besides," I add, "those expenses are down now that we're doing it ourselves again."

"That's the whole point," she says confidently.

I stare at her, blank.

"Look," she says, "Bee Man said to watch for money going out. Other than mortgage payments and utilities, property management is the biggest ongoing single expense. It goes out every month without fail, even if there's no maintenance required."

"Babe," I say. "*We're* doing that job now. It doesn't go out anymore."

Emma turns to me, exasperated. "I know that, Noah, but that's the *point*. It's a significant expense, now matter how you look at it."

I'm trying to be patient, but I'm still not getting it.

"It's what Tom was trying to tell you," she says. "We know how to do this work, *and* it's related to our core business. It's a significant cash outflow. Do you know what that means?"

I feel my mouth fall open.

"Exactly," Emma says. "We just found another stream."

—

Once we latch onto the idea, it's hard to let it go. Especially for Emma, she's like a dog with a bone.

There's a problem, however. We can't really run a property management business alone. We know how to do it, but we've already learned the hard way that we need to ask *who,* not *how.* So we have to hire someone, but we don't have the money to do that either.

"If we could get *customers,*" Emma says, "we can solve both problems. We get cash coming in, we use part of it to pay someone, and *voilà!* We have a business."

I think about my visit with Tom, about *synergies.*

I drag the laptop back in front of me. "What if," I begin, "the customers have been right in front of us this whole time?"

I pull up the websites for a few of the rental companies we've used to find tenants over the past couple of years.

"Look at all these people," I say. "The ones posting their available rentals. They're all similar to us. They all have management and maintenance needs, and they don't necessarily have the time or the skills." I'm typing, now, already in motion. "All we have to do is reach out to them and ask if they'd be interested in our services. Then we just hire someone to *do* it."

"Hello cash flow," Emma says.

"And," I add. "We'll have our *own* in-house property management. It was never cost-effective before, but if we have other customers . . ." I look at her with a smile.

"We can say goodbye to doing our own management and maintenance, and get paid for not doing it ourselves, too!" Emma finishes.

—

It takes longer than expected to get our first customer, but as Emma says, it's just a numbers game. If we contact enough property owners, eventually someone will say yes.

Sure enough, a few days and a few meetings later, we have our first contract. Our new service, Honeybee Property Management, will be managing a dozen units for a local developer.

For two months, it's an insane scramble with Emma and I taking care of everything. We're cutting grass and picking up rent checks and dealing with late-night power outages and leaks. Eventually, though, we hire a retired contractor, Dave, who's looking for part-time work. It's a perfect solution. He's great with people, he knows how to do almost everything, and he's got a lifetime of connections with local tradespeople.

With Dave now taking over the management of all the units, including our own, Emma is able to double down on her cold calls to other landlords. Within months, we add six more customers and another 60 units, and Dave is busy enough that we hire help for *him*.

Our newest stream of business is up and running.

—

It doesn't take long before I begin to see the other synergies the beekeeper was talking about. We're now effectively getting our own management done for a fraction of the cost, plus we have money rolling in each month from the other units we service.

On top of that, we realize that we can have Dave create preventative maintenance checks on our properties, and set up maintenance schedules. No more surprise roof leaks! In fact, it's so reassuring that we start selling the service to our client landlords as well. We now get those fees, plus we make a profit on the work that comes out of the inspections and maintenance plans. Our cash flow speeds up again.

Less than a year into the new line of business, another unexpected synergy materializes. One of our clients, the one with the dozen-unit apartment building, is planning to retire. He comes directly to us with a proposal: Do we want to buy his building? No real estate fees, and he'll finance most of the transaction.

Do we? *Hell yeah*!

That night, Emma and I go out for dinner for the first time since Buster's closed. I can feel the slippery slope leveling out.

"To us," I say, raising a glass of wine.

"And to Bee Man," Emma adds, with a smile.

—

The next few years pass in a blur. It's busy and occasionally stressful, but more than anything, it's *thrilling*. Our property management business has become an unexpected blockbuster. It was once a trickle but quickly became an enormous stream. It now supports 10 full-time employees.

The increased cash flow has let us buy a number of new income properties, too, a process that seems almost easy now that we have excellent property management in place. It's mainly a matter of a little math, combined with a lot of experience—both of which we can bring to the table thanks to our connected streams.

As our portfolio of multifamily properties grows, we realize there are more businesses *within* those businesses. We start to add streams of income within our apartment buildings and other complexes, things like laundry facilities, parking, and storage. We discover that we can resell other services like cable and tenant insurance, and take a portion of the revenue. We even install cell towers on several of our properties, and get a monthly stream from the telecom companies who use them.

A couple of years in, Dave approaches us with an idea. "I'm too young for this semi-retirement stuff," he says. "Why don't we move beyond the management and repairs and renovations, and actually build something new?"

Emma and I run it through what we call *the bee-filter*. Is it related to our core business? *Yes*. We can see the synergies. We understand Dave's business plan, and we know all the players. Will it create honey? *Yes*.

Six months later we break ground on a speculative custom home construction project. It sells before we even get the framing done. Six months after that, we start a small subdivision, pre-selling all 15 homes before we even service the lots.

The honey keeps flowing.

—

Another year passes in the blink of an eye. It feels like we're always hiring, always looking at deals, always solving problems. It's exhilarating.

Sometimes, when I get a few minutes of downtime, I think of Tom, and the bees. I think I should visit, maybe bring Emma, and maybe have another picnic. *That was so nice,* I think. But there are phones to answer, bills to pay, and streams to nurture. Tom slips from my mind, like water through my fingers, and I'm on to the next thing.

—

The streams grow, feeding off each other. We start to notice two trends. The first is that everyone keeps asking us how we do what we do. The second is we have a *lot* of cash.

Over the next six months, we start an online education business, teaching others how to buy and manage income properties. For a monthly subscription, our customers get video training and access to coaching resources and a growing online community. It turns out to be even more successful than we imagined. Being able to use the lessons we learned to give back to others is not only a natural fit, it's more rewarding than we imagined.

Next, we start a financing business, doing mortgages and bridge loans for real estate-related businesses. Our first clients? Well, they come from our online education business. *Synergies*, I think. The thought reminds me of Tom, and I briefly wonder how he's doing. Then the phone rings and the thought slips away.

The synergies become even more apparent when we start our syndication business, pooling the shared resources of groups of investors, so we can all invest in bigger projects than we would be able to on our own. The education platform feeds the syndication and mortgages. The mortgages, in turn, lend credibility to the education platform, which benefits even more from the shared knowledge and network of the syndicate. Never in my wildest dreams would I have imagined the synergies. The *possibilities*. So the streams grow, and the momentum builds. It's mayhem at times, but it works.

One evening, I look over our financial statements and realize our streams have grown and multiplied to an enormous degree. In fact, we're well past streams—we have a *river*.

Then the phone rings again. I look at the display: It's our real estate agent. I feel that little jolt of adrenaline and pick it up.

The river flows on.

13

THE FLOOD

It's been raining for days. An endless low-pressure system has settled over the state, and it's taking a toll. The city storm sewers are overloaded and the streets are awash with water. Beyond the city limits, crops sit in fields that look more like ponds.

The rain has effectively shut down every construction project we have in play. Most of my meetings have been canceled. Our online education platform is one of the only busy spots during all of this, but it's more or less on autopilot. So, while the forecast shows no relief, I find myself, for the first time in what feels like years, with time to *think*.

It doesn't take much thinking to know that I need to talk to Tom, badly. Truth be told, I'm not even sure what it is I want to talk *about*. Business is unbelievable. We just keep growing. Streams keep flowing, and the more momentum we get, the more things speed up. I realized at some point that Emma and I are millionaires many times over.

For all that, something is wrong. I need someone to talk to, and Tom is the only person I can think of. Emma thinks I shouldn't go.

Of course you don't, I think. It's a knee-jerk thought. I've been having them more and more often. But I catch myself before I say it aloud.

"I have to," I say, instead.

"*Fine,*" she says nothing further, just leaves the room, retreating to her office at the rear of the new house.

I watch her go, thinking I should say something. I hesitate, unsure. I grab my coat and head for the car instead.

—

For the first few minutes of the drive, I wonder if Emma is right. The wipers are barely keeping up with the onslaught. Maybe I should have stayed home.

I should just turn back, I think.

Instead, I keep driving. The rain seems to lessen up just a

bit, and I optimistically decide to push on. Within moments, however, the rain picks up again, hammering the windshield.

At least I have a dry, reliable car, I think. This isn't the kind of day you want to be stuck at the side of the road. With all that's going on, it might take hours to get a tow.

A memory surfaces: my first visit with Tom. *I was driving some piece of crap*, I recall. *The tire blew.* I chuckle. Now, I'm driving a luxury sedan that cost more than a year's pay at my old sales job. Remember that job? I was always trying to quit. And that crazy Duncan! What an *ass*.

Man, I think, *I don't miss those days.*

A smile crosses my face. Then realization hits me like a punch in the gut: I am missing those days. I'm actually longing for a time in life when I had a crappy car and a lousy job and Emma and I could barely make ends meet.

Emma. I shift uncomfortably in my seat. *I should have invited her.*

The thought makes me squirm, and so I tell myself the story I've been telling myself for over a year. I tell myself that I didn't invite her because she's busy. It's not entirely false. There are the kids, after all.

We have a boy and a girl, Nate and Ella. They're probably tearing the house apart right now. Although truth be told, that would take some doing. We moved into the new place when Emma was first pregnant. It's a lovely old mid-century modern home, sprawling, fully renovated, no expense spared—lots of space, lots of bedrooms. It's big enough that it would take two busy kids more than one rainy day to tear that place apart.

My story doesn't hold water for long. It's not about being busy. We have a full-time nanny, after all. The two kids would have been more than fine for a few hours while we visited Tom and Alice. The truth is, I don't *want* Emma to come. I want the time alone. I need to think.

And you aren't getting along, a voice in my head says.

No. We aren't.

And this visit to Tom isn't about business, the voice says.

No. It isn't. This visit feels different somehow.

A sudden, blaring honk startles me from my thoughts. I've been slowly drifting into the next lane. A car swerves away from me, and speeds ahead, the rain hissing from its tires.

I need to straighten this out, I think.

—

It's still raining when I pull up Tom's lane. I stop the car part way, looking out over the landscape. Through the rainy windshield, I can see the multiple streams flow down the hill. In the rain, they're now raging torrents, flowing into one rushing river. The water has eroded the banks, and as I watch, an enormous chunk of sod crashes into the river and is quickly washed down to the pond.

The pond itself is almost twice its normal size. Water is pouring over the far side, flooding the woods beyond. There's no sign of the deer.

I drive past the house and stop in front of the garage. One of the bay doors is open, and I see Tom standing just inside, sheltered from the rain next to the old Ford. He lifts a hand as I pull up. I step out and jog through the puddles, into the shelter of the garage and the warmth of the beekeeper's home.

———

Tom's handshake is as firm as ever, but he looks older. Then again, it's been nearly five years since I've seen him. I probably look different, too. As if reading my mind, he looks me over and nods his chin in the direction of my midsection.

"You get back into the restaurant business?" he asks with a chuckle.

"Very funny," I say, patting my gut. "I guess honey has more calories than I thought."

Tom laughs. "Sit down," he says. "I'll make coffee."

He busies himself behind the bar, and as he grinds beans and measures grounds, I tell him the story of the last five years. How we put his lessons to work. How our streams grew, and merged, and grew again. How we built something that exceeded our wildest dreams. How we became wealthy in a way that Emma and I had never expected. How amazing it all is. How *perfect*.

I realize I'm talking too much. I sip my coffee, sweetened with a little honey, just like I remember, and we sit and watch the rain. Tom nods at the huge windows, the rain streaming down in tiny rivulets.

"I'd offer you a ride in the Ford," he says, "but the old road's a mess back there. We'd never get home."

I picture the old barn and the hive boxes in the clearing. I ask, "What do the bees do in all this?"

"Oh, the bees are just fine," Tom says. "They just hunker down. They'll make honey tomorrow. Makes no difference to them."

"I guess being a bee is pretty simple," I say.

I watch the rain, and I'm reminded of another rainy day, years ago, when I was still working for Duncan. I'd sat in a meeting on a wet day like this, and I'd wondered, *what's the point?*

"Sometimes I wonder if it might be nice to be a bee," I say, absently. "You just show up, make the honey, and go to bed. Rinse and repeat."

Tom sips his coffee. There's a long, silent pause. Finally, he says, "Well. I reckon if you were so darn happy making honey, you wouldn't have driven halfway across the state in the worst rain in 50 years. What's up?"

I stare at him, my eyes wide. Then we both break into broad grins. As always, the beekeeper seems to have a way of getting to the heart of things.

I take a deep breath. "Truth be told," I say, "things maybe aren't exactly perfect."

—

It feels good to tell it, to unload what's been weighing so heavily on me. Tom feels like the perfect person to unburden myself to. We're close, but not that close. He's wise, but not judgmental.

So I tell him all of it. How Emma and I have grown apart. How I've lost track of my friends and my hobbies. How maybe I feel a little tired sometimes, a little lost.

"And yes," I say, patting my stomach with a grimace, "I've put on a little weight."

The kids, I tell him, are amazing. A lot of work, but they're the one bright spot.

"The trouble is," I tell Tom, "I just feel like we don't have time to be the best parents. I mean I never thought that I'd be the guy with the live-in nanny, but I *am* that guy."

"Maybe that's fine," Tom suggests.

"That's the thing," I say, running my hands through my hair. "It *is* fine. It just isn't how we pictured our life. I thought I'd be a real hands-on dad: home a lot, changing diapers, never missing a ball game."

Tom steps out from behind the bar. "Come over here," he says.

We walk to the enormous glass wall that fronts the house. Tom points at where the streams converge, creating what is, with the rain, a rushing torrent. Even since I arrived, I see that the river has changed course. More of the bank has disappeared, the bend has deepened, and the water is faster.

"Streams change as they grow," Tom says. "They find their own course. They do things you don't expect. The bigger they grow, the more they change the things around them. If they get big enough, they have a way of sweeping things away."

I watch as another clump of earth breaks away from the bank and flows downstream.

"But I thought the whole point was to grow the streams," I say.

"Ah," Tom replies, "right."

He looks through the glass, and up at the dark clouds.

"You know," he says, "I think maybe we oughta head outside after all."

—

Ten minutes later we're walking out of Tom's open garage and into a steady downpour. I'm wearing borrowed boots, a raincoat, and a hat, but even with all the gear I can tell I'll be soaked before too long. Tom doesn't seem to notice. He heads off into the rain, marching with steady determination.

"It's pretty wet out here," I call out, raising my voice over the noise of the rain.

I can't tell if he hears me or not, but he keeps walking anyway. After a moment I give in and follow him down the driveway, and out onto the broad expanse of lawn.

Tom leads me to the point where the smaller streams merge into the river. Now that I'm standing beside the rushing water, I get a true sense of just how fast it's moving. What has always been a placid stream is now muddy and churning, almost rapids.

"Wow," I say. "It's really moving."

"It's funny," Tom says. "A week ago the grass was dying. We were in a drought. I was practically praying for rain."

"Looks like you got it," I say.

"Yep. Careful what you wish for," he says.

Tom stands, silent, watching the torrent flow past us. Then it hits me.

"You're not really talking about the rain," I say.

I can see the smile tugging at the corners of his mouth. A sad smile, perhaps.

I watch the river flow.

"Did you ever wonder," I ask Tom, not taking my eyes off the water, "why you did it all? Built all this?"

There's a long Tom-pause, and I wonder if perhaps I've offended him.

"That's the difference between us and bees," he says, at last. "They just do the work. They don't have to think about *why* they make the honey."

"I guess not," I say. "They need it to survive."

"That's part of it, to be sure," Tom says. "But it's deeper than that. Bees are wired to just make honey. It's instinctual. It's how they're built. They don't get a choice in the matter."

"Are you saying bees don't have existential crises?" I ask.

Tom laughs. "Call it what you want," he chuckles, "but that's the difference. For us, for *people*, just making honey isn't enough."

I feel a cold rivulet of water run down my back.

"What do you mean?" I ask.

Tom surveys the rushing torrent of water, then squints up into the rain.

"Maybe we should check on the hives," he says.

—

A short but muddy walk later, I'm soaking wet and standing next to Tom in the clearing behind the barn. The bees, he assures me, are fine. I'm getting the feeling we're really not here to check the hives.

"Do you remember," Tom asks, "your first stream?"

"How could I forget?" I reply. "We rented out our basement. We were so excited."

Tom nods. "Why did you do it?"

I think back to those early days. "I was desperate to leave my job," I say. "I felt stuck. Like we'd always be on the treadmill, always trying to make ends meet." I think back to working for Duncan. "I think I really wanted the freedom. I wanted to feel like I had a choice."

"And now?" Tom asks.

"I guess," I pause, considering. "I guess we accomplished that. I left that job years ago. Now, we're financially free. If we just stopped today, we'd be fine. The kids, our retirement, it's all taken care of."

"So," Tom says, turning to look at me. "Why are you still doing it?"

The question catches me off guard. I turn toward him, and the rivulet of rain running down my back picks up speed and begins to drizzle straight down my pants. I barely notice. I just stand there, unmoving, the rain soaking my face. *Because,* I realize, *I don't know why.*

"Do you remember," Tom asks, "the second lesson I taught you?"

I think back. "About finding surplus," I say. "Every stream has a source." I flash back to my insight that we could rent our basement. It seems so long ago.

"Right," Tom says. "On the surface, that's about assets and putting them to work. About leveraging your cash, or the things you own, or your time and talent, to create your first stream.

"But," he continues. "There's another lesson there. Every stream needs a source, but that source runs deeper than just the business and the cash flow. When you started out, you had a reason to start a business. You had a *why.* That was the *real* source that drove your first streams, and everything that followed. It was that energy."

He nods at the hives, sitting silently, rain pooling on the lids.

"The bees don't need a *why.* They just do it. It doesn't matter how much honey they have; they just keep making it. People, on the other hand, we need a *why.* When the *why* runs out," he turns to me, "we lose a little piece of ourselves."

With those words, it's as if a final puzzle piece has fallen into place. Like I've just unlocked some deep, ancient mystery, and now, somewhere hidden from view, a long-dormant piece of machinery is coming to life.

"Are you saying I need to find a new *why?*" I ask.

"I'm saying that just making honey isn't a purpose," Tom says. "You're not a bee, Noah. For all the things that bees teach us, we're still human. And as humans, we need more than honey. We need a *why.*"

I stand there beside the beekeeper, the rain running down my face.

It's so obvious. We lost our *why.* We were running our business on autopilot. We just kept making more honey for the sake of it, reinvesting it to make even more honey. We were creating a river with no end, no banks, no boundaries.

For what? I have no idea.

—

I'm not sure how long I've been standing when I realize that Tom is speaking to me.

"I'm sorry," I say. "I was thinking."

"Did you hear that?" the beekeeper asks.

"What?" I blink, not understanding.

Then it hits me: *The rain has stopped.*

I wipe my face, clearing my eyes. I listen again.

To the west, the clouds are thinning. The light in the clearing changes and I look up the sky. As clouds part, I catch a glimpse of blue sky. Then, the sun emerges. At first it's just a hazy circle, then it emerges in full force. I feel the warmth of it.

I turn to Tom, "It's clear—"

"Shhh," he says. "Just listen."

We stand still, silent, in the clearing, the sun drying our faces. I can feel the heat build in the ground as the sun hits it. A fine mist starts to rise. I turn to Tom, raising my eyebrows, a silent question. He nods, knowingly. Lays a finger to his lips. *Shhh.* I listen. I realize I'm squinting my eyes, like I'm trying to see farther than my vision allows.

Then I hear it, faint and soft, like distant conversation: It's the hum of bees.

—

Tom stands beside the old Ford. He holds a jar of honey in his weathered hands.

"I don't know how to thank you . . ." I struggle to find the words, "for everything."

He just nods, then hands me the jar. "This batch is particularly sweet," he says. "I reckon it's worth savoring."

I look at him, trying to decipher the meaning, but his lined face is inscrutable.

"Be well, Noah," he says. "Be well."

He shakes my hand firmly, turns, and walks inside.

I climb in my car, fighting back inexplicable tears. Then I set the jar on the seat and I drive. And I think. And I drive. When I see the first towers of the city skyline on the horizon, I pull over, and I open the jar of honey.

14

THE BEEKEEPER'S LAST LESSON

It's the first bee of the season. Well, maybe not the first, but it's the first one I've seen. That means today is Bee Day.

Like so many great things, the tradition started with Emma. It was a beautiful, late spring day, and she spotted a bee wobbling its way around a wildflower, one of many flowers that the kids had planted at the main entrance. She named the bee "Tom," and it stuck like glue. Now, each spring we wait for the sighting of the first bee. Whoever sees "Tom" first gets to ring the school bell and make the announcement: No more classes today.

So far this spring, the bell has been silent, which means I'll be the one to announce Bee Day. I know from experience there will be absolute, joyous pandemonium. For the moment, I just sit and watch the bee, enjoying the silence.

As the bee trundles around the flower, growing heavy with pollen and nectar, I turn my face to the sun. I'm reminded of my first meeting with the real Tom, and how the old bee-keeper had rescued me from a flat tire and a rainstorm. When the sun had come out at his beautiful home, I had turned to it in just the same way.

He rescued you from more than the rain, I think.

It was true. I was so frustrated then. That job I hated, our struggles to pay the bills, and underneath it all, something deeper and darker: A sense of *is this all there is?*

Tom taught us so much.

I think back to another sunny day. The first time we'd come to this very spot—Emma, the kids, and I. There was nothing here, then. We'd parked at the edge of the road and hiked into what was just a forest.

A few minutes into the walk, we'd found a small river, fed by multiple streams that seemed to emerge from some deep, hidden source beneath the earth. I'd looked at Emma. She raised her eyebrows. Cautious optimism.

A little further on, we'd spied an opening through the trees. We left the cool shade of the forest, walking into the heat of the warm sun, and an enormous meadow scattered with wildflowers.

We stood there, scanning the field. From somewhere behind me, I heard Ella's voice: "Look Nate! *A bumbler-bee!*"

I looked at Emma. "I think this is it," I said.

She had smiled, then, and taken my hand.

"This is definitely it."

—

That was 10 years ago. Ella and Nate are in college now. Emma and I are empty nesters. Or hivers? It doesn't matter; we're hardly alone. We have each other, and our marriage has never been stronger. Just as important, *we have this place.*

I watch as Tom the bee finishes with the flower. His legs loaded with pollen, he lifts off, zigging and zagging away from me in a complex pattern, one that I know carries a message to his fellow bees.

I hear the voice of the beekeeper in my ears: *You can learn a lot from bees.*

In the distance, the sound of children's laughter bubbles up, and I turn. Once again, I'm struck by what I see, and a smile lights my face. The school isn't large, at least, not yet, but it's beautiful. In its sweeping lines, I see the influence Tom and Alice's home has had on the place: plenty of glass, lots of sun, and room to grow.

The room to grow is important. Emma and I still have

many plans for this place. I bid farewell to the bee as it meanders away, and head for my office.

—

The truth is, I don't really *have* a job here. Our team, the teachers, the principal, and the staff, they're all amazing to the point that I'm pretty much redundant. I keep an office nonetheless. The more time passes, the more and more Emma and I find ourselves here. I like the energy. I like the kids.

I like the *why*.

I sit down at my desk. Through my window, I see the hives of the apiary. A couple of 10-year-olds are struggling their way into pint-sized bee suits, helped by a teacher. I'm reminded, once more, of Tom.

The beekeeper passed away last year. My only regret is that he didn't live to see this place: the laughing children streaming inside when the bell rings, the apiary with its collection of hives. The honey provides a little income for the school, but more important, beekeeping gives us a teaching tool that the kids love, and one that *works*. The students leave this place prepared for the future in a way they never could be otherwise.

I reach down and open the lower drawer of my desk. Inside is a jar of honey. Long empty, its label is now yellowed with age. I spin off the top and stick my nose close to the glass. I catch the faintest whiff of something sweet, like the ghost of some memory. I smile and I turn the lid over.

The words are still clear, almost a decade after I first read them, during that week of torrential rains. On the day the sun, and my understanding, broke through the clouds.

- -

Lesson 6: Create Streams of Purpose
Money isn't your reason; it only funds it

Streams of purpose. That was Tom's final gift to us. Create streams of purpose.

Once Emma and I found ours, there was no stopping us. Once we had a reason, a *why*, for our work, things grew exponentially. Our relationship grew stronger. Our family grew closer. Everything—health, wealth, happiness—it all grew, and continues to. All thanks to Tom.

And Alice, of course. She is still alive and well, and sparky as ever. She was here for the opening. She cut the ribbon, standing beneath the enormous stone arch chiseled with the words that would define our purpose: The Honeybee Academy.

The school was a natural fit for us from day one. We'd already learned so much about education from our own real estate training platform, we knew we could bring our success to young people and make a difference that couldn't happen any other way. Plus, our experience in business meant we were well equipped to run a nonprofit in the most efficient way possible.

Since opening day, the school has doubled from its modest beginnings, then doubled again. There is a gymnasium now, and, by next year, a full residence where international students seeking refuge from troubled nations can be sponsored to live and study for free. Like all the kids here, they'll learn not just the standard school curriculum, but also a curriculum for *life*—one inspired by Tom's lessons.

"Honey for your thoughts?" says a voice.

I look up to see Emma standing in the door. There is gray in her hair now. A few more smile lines on her face. They've given her what, to me, is a deep and lasting beauty.

"Hey there, queen bee," I say.

She laughs. "I'd call you a worker bee, but it looks to me like you're just daydreaming."

"I saw Tom," I say. Even as it comes out of my mouth, I'm not sure if I mean the first bee of the season, or the beekeeper himself. There are times when I feel he's here—watching, nodding, and smiling silently.

Emma sees the jar in my hands. She walks to my desk, sits in my lap, and puts her arms around my neck.

"I guess this is Bee Day," she says. "Things are about to get crazy."

"Let's just wait. Just a little longer."

Emma leans her head against mine, and we sit,

holding each other. The sun streams in the window. The laughter of children floats on the air.

I look down at the jar in my hand. It's empty, but the real sweetness, the lesson that Tom and the bees taught us, remains.

- -

THE END

THE BEEKEEPER'S LESSONS

1. Escape the Honey Trap
Transactions don't create wealth, equity does

2. Find Your Surplus
Every stream has a source

3. Make It Happen
Every source of honey comes with a few stings; the best antidote is action.

4. Build Your Hive
Learn to ask 'who' instead of 'how'

5: Commit to Your Core
The best streams feed each other

6: Create Streams of Purpose
Money isn't your reason; it only funds it

TIME FOR ACTION

Putting the Beekeeper's Principles to Work

- What drives you to want streams of income?

- What does money mean to you?

- How can you give back, now and in the future, in ways that are meaningful to you?

WWW.JAKEANDGINO.COM/HONEYBEE

AFTERWORD

Noah and the rest of the characters in this book may be fiction, but there's a *big* dose of reality here, too. Every lesson in these pages comes from our own real-life experience.

Those lessons were hard won. We learned them the painful way: by trying our best and making mistakes. We were often rejected, and even more often unsure, but we always tried to move forward. We were frequently told we'd never succeed.

One of our first deals was a property called The Shamrock Motel. "Motel" was a generous description: It was really a motley collection of cottages, efficiency units, and duplexes that we tried to shape into something that worked.

Like the characters in this story, we started out doing almost everything ourselves—in fact, a *lot* of our early surplus came from Jake managing the property himself. It was a lot of hard work and there were a lot of stings. The septic drain field failed six months after we bought it. One tenant sued us for bed bugs—in *their* furniture. We had to evict our weekly tenants to help get rid of drugs on the property. At one point, a tenant *died* in a unit. Sometimes it was overwhelming.

It was more than worth it in the end. That first property brought us some surplus cash flow, and it appreciated in value. We were able to refinance it, pull our money out, and add more streams. Like Noah and Emma, those streams eventually gained momentum.

Challenges, rejection, and uncertainty are all part of creating streams of income. They come with the territory. When you learn to treat those things as problems that you can lean into and solve head-on, you also learn that you're capable of far more than you think.

Like Noah, we also made some bad choices. We had some Buster's Bistro problems of our own. Gino got into a mobile home park deal with a friend and lost a substantial amount of money and time. The reason? A lack of due diligence, experience, and education. Gino trusted someone he didn't know well, and invested in a business he didn't fully understand. It was a disaster.

In those moments, it's tempting to blame your partner, or the deal, or any number of external issues. But just like Buster's Bistro, the real problem isn't anyone else. The person responsible is always you.

Which brings us to this: The hidden lesson of this book is that Noah and Emma find success not because of great luck or talent, but because of *education*. What the Beekeeper is really teaching them, lesson by lesson, is that success inevitably comes from improving *yourself*. If you want to earn more, then learn more. If you want a better life, focus on making *yourself* better.

If you take away anything from this book, we hope it's this*: Keep trying to get better.* At the end of the day, that's what makes the honey flow. More importantly, it always makes for a sweeter life.

Thanks for reading,

—Jake & Gino

STREAMS OF
GIVING BACK

Since we made our first investment in 2013, we've amassed over 1,500 units of multifamily real estate worth $100 million.

Along the way, much like the characters in this story, we discovered a true passion for giving back. That led us to founding Rand Cares, a charitable organization focused on feeding hungry children.

Tom, the beekeeper in the story, had a lifelong passion for giving back in the form of mentoring and education, and so do we. Like our fictional Bee Man, we've dedicated a great deal of time to teaching others about the power of the lessons in this book.

To hear more inspiring stories about how others have found financial freedom through multiple streams of income, try our free podcast, *Jake and Gino: Multifamily Real Estate Investing & More* at www.jakeandgino.com.

Keep the honey flowing,

—Jake & Gino

APPENDIX A

Notes on Complementary Streams of Income

Every business is different, just like every person's life is unique. Your streams, as they grow, will be your own, and there's no formula that fits everyone.

However, it's important to understand that this book is primarily about *complementary* streams of income. Those are streams of income that support and feed each other based on the idea of synergies that the beekeeper taught Noah. In other words, multiple complementary streams of income are very different from multiple unrelated businesses.

To help make decisions about what streams could connect in your future, there are a few different lenses to look at them through—common ways in which complementary streams tend to evolve. Those lenses can create a helpful framework for asking yourself questions about where your next stream might come from.

Lens #1: Business Services

In the story, Noah and Emma find their first complementary stream by analyzing where their cash is flowing *out*. Anything you pay for regularly as a service for your existing business could become a possible stream of income.

A restaurateur, for example, spends a lot on dishes, glassware, linens, and all the other many supplies it takes to run a restaurant. He might consider starting a restaurant supply service. He can then provide that service to every restaurant in town, generate profits, and save money on his own use of the service.

Some generalized examples might include:

- Office support services
- Inventory and raw material sales and supply
- Accounting, legal, and other professional services
- Management
- Maintenance and repair
- Certification and inspection

These are all services a business might use regularly that could be turned into new streams of income.

Questions to ask yourself:

- Where does my money flow out to?
- What does my competition spend a lot on?
- What things would be cheaper if they were scaled up?

Lens #2: Education

As you become more experienced, it's only natural to want to share that wisdom with others. And trust us, once you start to gain momentum, you're going to get questions!

This combination of you getting wiser, and people wanting to learn from you presents an opportunity for other streams, like:

- Books
- Video training
- Membership education websites
- Coaching
- Consulting

Questions to ask yourself:

- What are my areas of expertise?
- What do I do better than most people?
- What questions do I answer time and time again?

Lens #3: Finance

In the beginning, finding money to get streams up and running is often a big challenge. As you grow, however, your cash flow grows with you. You may find yourself in a position to be on the other side of the table, putting your surplus cash to use in new ways:

- Bridge financing
- Private mortgages
- Hard money lending

Questions to ask yourself:

- Who in my industry is always looking for money?
- What types of businesses and deals do I have experience in analyzing?
- How can I put my surplus cash to work?

Stream Examples

Our students find it helpful to see practical examples of complementary streams in different industries.

Here are a few examples of multiple streams of income that might spin out of one core job or profession:

Realtor

- Real Estate Sales
- Insurance company
- Fix & Flip projects
- Buy & Hold rentals
- Money-lending
- Education/writing books
- Title company
- Accountant services
- Inspection Company
- Construction Company

Restaurateur

- Food supply
- Food equipment supply
- Retail and commercial packaged foods
- Cookbooks and training
- Staff and owner training
- Restaurant startup financing

Auto Mechanic

- Car sales

- Vehicle detailing

- Vehicle financing

- Licensing and certification

- Rentals and leasing

- Advertising/vehicle wrapping

APPENDIX B

Notes on Multifamily Real Estate

Our core business is multifamily real estate. Those are properties like apartment buildings, condominiums, multiplexes, and mobile home parks.

Part of the reason we love this industry so much is that it lends itself to *many* complementary streams.

Multiple Streams of Revenue in Multifamily

- Investment
- Property Management
- Education
- Syndication
- Service Company
- Construction Company
- Consulting Company

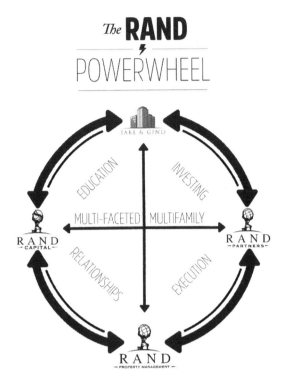

Like Noah and Emma, we discovered that there were also many lucrative streams *inside* our multifamily businesses, like:

- Laundry
- Cable Contracts
- Storage
- Parking
- Cell Towers
- Short-term rentals

- Utility bill back to tenant
- Pet fees
- Late fees
- Application fees
- Renter's insurance

For us, there's no better business than multifamily real estate!

If you'd like to learn from experts with a successful multifamily track record, you can learn more about our multifamily mentorship program at: www.jakeandgino.com/honeybee

Team Building

Over the years, we've developed a long list of roles for team members and preferred vendors. Many of these are real estate specific, but there's a lot of overlap with other businesses:

- Coach/Mentor
- Laundry
- Cable
- Attorney/Title Company
- Accountant
- Real Estate Broker
- Property Manager

- Mortgage Broker
- Banker
- Insurance Agent
- Maintenance/ Contractors
- Inspector
- Architect
- Website developer

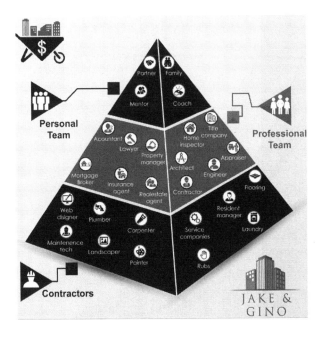

A few things that are important to remember as you build out your team:

- You don't need to find or hire all these people at once. What you *do* need to make sure you do is always think of your streams of income as businesses. That means you'll need to build a team over time.

- You don't always need to hire full time. Your team can include employees, but it can also include vendors, service providers, part-timers, and contractors.

- Often the first team member is the hardest. That's where you make the big leap from doing everything yourself to delegating. Start as small as you need to!

ABOUT THE AUTHORS

 **Jake Stenziano**, MBA, spent 10 years performing various roles in the Pharmaceutical and Biotech industry before actively pursuing multifamily investments in 2010. Since then he has acquired nearly 1,500 multifamily units with his partners. Jake enjoys running the day-to-day operations of Rand Property Management LLC.

He has worked with brokers, sellers, title insurers, appraisers, engineers, architects, property management software companies, attorneys, lenders, equity partners, insurance companies, leasing and property management teams; negotiated terms for new leases, renewals, and RUBS; ensured compliance and tenant billing; and hired employees in property management. He also has extensive experience with acquisition analysis and due diligence.

Jake is the host of the number one multifamily podcast on iTunes and has a best-selling book on multifamily investing, *Wheelbarrow Profits*. Jake and his family reside in Knoxville, Tennessee.

Gino Barbaro is an investor, business owner, author, coach, and entrepreneur. He is the co-founder of Jake & Gino, a multi-family real estate education company that offers coaching and training in real estate, founded upon their proprietary framework of "Buy Right, Manage Right & Finance Right."

Gino is the best-selling author of two books, *Wheelbarrow Profits* and *Family, Food and the Friars*. Gino graduated from IPEC (Institute for Professional Excellence in Coaching) where he earned his designation as a Certified Professional Coach. He currently resides in St. Augustine, Florida, with his beautiful wife Julia and their six children: Gabriella, Michael, Sofia, Veronica, Cecilia, and Laura.